A Debate on
A TIME TO CHOOSE

A Debate on
A TIME TO CHOOSE

A CRITIQUE
William Tavoulareas

A REPLY
Carl Kaysen

Ballinger Publishing Company • Cambridge, Massachusetts
A Subsidiary of J.B. Lippincott Company

This book is printed on recycled paper.

Library of Congress Cataloging in Publication Data

Tavoulareas, William.
  The energy debate.
  "An energy policy publication of the Ford Foundation."
  Includes bibliographical references.
  1. Energy policy—United States. 2. Ford Foundation. Energy Policy Project.
A time to choose. I. Kaysen, Carl, joint author. II. Title.
HD9502.U52T38   333.7'0973   77-24059
ISBN 0-88410-070-7

Contents

Marshall Robinson, Vice-President, Ford Foundation

Part I

A Time to Choose: A Critique

William P. Tavoulareas, President, Mobil Corp.

Why a publication to balance *A Time to Choose*
became necessary.

Energy policy must include supply policy; conservation alone
is not enough. *A Time to Choose* is a defective blueprint for
cutting energy usage, and it does not consider all the costs.

The resources and technology of the U.S. provide great opportunities to avoid the high economic, social and political costs of
suppressed consumption.

Failure to understand the complex dynamics of supplying and
consuming energy opens the way to counterproductive use of
the issue for partisan political purposes.

Government decisions would replace those of consumers
and business, but it would be an elitist bureaucracy since
it would not permit consumer and business voices to be
heard.

The amount of easy conservation has been overstated and
the costs of reducing consumption understated.

Allegations, innuendo, and imagery do not constitute
evidence.

The consequences of an energy undernourished economy are
greater than they appear in *A Time to Choose*.

Part II

A Reply
Carl Kaysen

David W. Skinner Professor of Political Economy
Massachusetts Institute of Technology

List of Figures

List of Tables

Foreword

In December 1971 the trustees of the Ford Foundation authorized the organization of the Energy Policy Project.

In subsequent decisions the trustees approved supporting appropriations to a total of $4 million, which was spent over a three-year period. The project published twenty volumes of studies and reports by authorities in a wide range of fields. The final report of that project, *A Time to Choose*, is the document discussed in this volume.

The foreword to *A Time to Choose* described the organization of the Energy Policy Project and noted that responsibility for the report's content was vested in the director, David Freeman. The project also had an advisory board representing a wide range of opinion on energy matters, and although the board was a purely advisory unit, the opinions and information provided by its members were helpful to the director and his staff. Each member of the advisory board was assured of the right to have separate comments published as a part of the final report. W. P. Tavoulareas, president of Mobil Oil Corporation, was a member of the advisory board.

Mr. Tavoulareas expressed dissatisfaction with the amount of space made available for his comments: he reminded us that in inviting him to serve on the advisory board the Foundation had said nothing about a space limitation on any comments he might offer for publication in the final report—yet the advisory board did set such a limit; he also argued that the heavy emphasis in *A Time to Choose* on oil- and gas-related matters made it difficult for him to respond fully within the limited amount of space allocated to his remarks in that book and that as the only oil company executive on the advisory board he had a special responsibility for comment. The foundation did not overrule the advisory board's self-imposed limit on the length of its members' comments in *A Time to Choose*, but the foundation did agree subsequently to publish Mr. Tavoulareas's full statement, which follows. At the same time, in order to give the reader the benefit of more than one perspective, the foundation asked another member of the advisory board, Dr. Carl Kaysen, David W. Skinner professor of political economy at MIT and former director of the Institute of Advanced Study, to review Mr. Tavoulareas's statement and to make whatever comments he considered appropriate. We hope that the remarks of Mr. Tavoulareas and Dr. Kaysen will serve the interests of wider debate and enlightenment about energy policy.

Marshall Robinson
Vice-President
Office of Resources and the Environment
Ford Foundation

Part I

A Time to Choose: A Critique

William P. Tavoulareas

Preface

The publication of *A Time to Choose* marked the conclusion of the Energy Policy Project (EPP), an effort that required years and cost the Ford Foundation $4 million. *A Time to Choose* was intended to clarify energy policy options and to aid in reaching the difficult decisions needed to reconcile new energy policies with other national objectives. The president of the Ford Foundation, in a preface to an earlier publication of the Energy Policy Project, aptly noted the need to "set the issues of national policy in a general framework which can assist citizens and their representatives in reaching balanced judgments."[a] Unfortunately, the final report of the project, *A Time to Choose*, did not live up to the objectives which were so laudably set forth by the president of the foundation. Space limitations for advisory board comments made it impossible for me to develop an opposing point of view in detail.[b]

Other board members were critical of some aspects of the report,

[a]Ford Foundation Energy Policy Project, *Exploring Energy Choices* (A Preliminary Report) (1974), p. i.

[b]While I objected to space limitations for my own comments, I should make it clear that I would endorse a more generous use of space for *any* other advisory board member; freedom to comment was one of the key conditions of advisory board membership at the time the board was organized by the foundation. Every board member must necessarily have resolved in his own mind how extensive his comments needed to be, but for my part a limitation of six double-spaced typewritten pages was hardly adequate to comment on the results of two-and-a-half years of work, which gave rise to a report of nearly 450 printed pages (excluding advisory board comments) and over 1000 printed pages of supplementary studies.

but brief critical comments were sometimes neutralized by a generalized "pat on the back" later in the same piece. Thus, for example, two members of the board did call attention to analytical deficiencies by saying: "The populist speech writer seems at times to have taken over from the analyst," but the same statement then went on to say, "despite these reservations, *we consider the report an important document and its major propositions worth the serious concern of the country*" (emphasis added).

It is our intent, in this publication, to make a positive contribution to the debate over how to resolve America's continuing crisis of choice over its energy policy. A critical evaluation of *A Time to Choose* is exceedingly difficult because the EPP final report is *not* an integrated document that examines costs and benefits of options; therefore, it *cannot* assist citizens and their representatives in reaching balanced judgments. Costs and benefits are not a matter only of dollars and BTUs but also involve subjects as diverse as the quality of the environment, the organization of government and business institutions, and, most important, freedom of consumer choice.

The subject matter of the report is complex enough to defy the comprehension of many under the best of circumstances, but the project made matters worse by utilizing a presentation format that has served to confuse the public perception of the message of the report and to camouflage the seriousness of its recommendations. Instead of forecasting energy consumption in the U.S., the report adopts the concept of estimating what future energy consumption *would be* if Americans continued their consumption patterns of the recent past. Since conditions never remain the same for very long, this technique seriously complicates any effort to compare the project's "Historical Growth" scenario with other published forecasts of energy consumption, all of which *do* recognize the effects of changing conditions. While the staff and the advisory board fully understood the technique being utilized, some members of both groups chose to ignore the distinction between an extension of past trends and a forecast of the future, with the result that they play down the size of the necessary reductions in consumption required by the policies that the project advocates.

From the outset, the project had focused on discouraging consumption, while essentially neglecting the issue of supply. As the only advisor from a petroleum company, my objection to the direction the project took was published in its preliminary report.[c] Throughout the life of the project no attention was paid to my

---

[c]*Exploring Energy Choices*, p. 57.

pleas that the costs of restricting consumption be fully examined and compared with the options for expanding supplies.

In the following pages, we will demonstrate that *A Time to Choose* is not a reasonable basis for deliberations leading to the formulation of national energy policy. In doing so, we shall also briefly describe the available—and we think more acceptable—alternative. It is encouraging that those who have reviewed the factual basis for our line of reasoning have found, for the most part, little of substance to criticize, even though their rhetoric would imply a contrary conclusion.[d]

[d]This comment is particularly applicable to some who were intimately familiar with the process by which *A Time to Choose* was prepared, either as an advisory board member or as a part of the project staff.

Overview

The essence of America's energy problem is that the availability and cost of present and future energy supplies are uncertain. The policies required to solve this problem were to have been the subject of *A Time to Choose*. Instead, the report assumes energy supplies would not be a difficult problem at any level of demand; indeed, it postulates various possible mixes of supply sources. By deciding to ignore the already declining U.S. oil and natural gas production and the implication of increased dependence on foreign imports to fill the energy gap, the Energy Policy Project was left with only a "conservation" methodology. But conservation as used in *A Time to Choose* goes far beyond the elimination of obvious waste and rational adjustment to higher prices; it becomes an end unto itself. Conservation alone cannot solve our energy problem, even if it is defined in the extreme terms of a complete halt to further growth in energy usage. Energy supplies are being used up, and *A Time to Choose* provides no clues as to what is needed to replace these supplies, or to find new sources. Indeed, some of its recommendations would block development of new supplies. U.S. oil and natural gas production is declining. Growth in both the production and usage of coal is retarded by environmental problems. Nuclear energy is beset by regulatory, licensing, financing, and environmental difficulties. Long lead times are required to gain access to new sources of supply and to solve some of these problems. Conservation does deserve high priority, but supply policy is even more urgent.

Even real zero growth would require that supplies being used up be replaced by new sources, but without supplies there can be no choice; conservation must become coercion and rationing. On the other hand, if policies allowed the development of new supplies the consumer would have *time* to select an appropriate balance of conservation and consumption. Our contention that the consumer should have the choice between these alternatives—and the time in which to make such a choice—is precisely the sharpest point of disagreement we have with *A Time to Choose*. Even today, in 1977, there continue to be those who urge, in essence, that we decide *now* to limit consumption and *wait until later* to see whether—and what—supplies should be made available.

Even the casual reader will recognize that *A Time to Choose* is intended as a blueprint for reduced future energy consumption and imposition of forced life-styles by narrowing the range of alternatives. But it is an inadequate blueprint both because of internal technical faults and because the cost estimates based upon it are understated. It does not comprehend the full cost to the economy and to the personal aspirations of all individuals seeking to improve their standard of living. Even more significantly, *A Time to Choose* designs the wrong structure. Its concept of conservation goes beyond the elimination of waste and the requirements of rational economic decisions and results in pervasive restrictions on individual choice mandated by government. Unfortunately, rational conservation—even when supplemented by the mandates specified in *A Time to Choose*—is not enough to eliminate the basic energy problem. Energy demands not only continue to grow, but *also* new sources of energy would be required to replace those consumed in the next twenty-five years, under any of the project's scenarios. A policy that focuses disproportionately on reducing consumption is essentially a policy of despair, and carries substantial risk of creating even greater problems in the future. A policy of despair is not necessary in a country with the resources and technology of the U.S.

Not until 1973 did this nation really become aware of the energy problem. For years we had been increasing oil imports without considering whether we might become over-reliant on these supplies or the effect these additional demands would have upon the price of foreign oil and on our balance of payments. During those years adjustment to our nation's increased interest in protection of the environment resulted in extensive delays in production schedules of every energy source. The result: a growing gap between production and consumption which could only be filled by imports or shortage. For the future the issue is still how to narrow that gap; emphasis on conservation alone only aggravates the problem. Determining

America's future energy policy must involve an examination of both demand and supply; *A Time to Choose* does not do this. *A Time to Choose* stresses reduced growth in consumption, yet even its radical limits on consumption would not prevent some growth in demand. But where are the supplies to come from? To help define the real and continuing nature of the problem, my company, Mobil, ran a two-part message in *The New York Times* of January 26, 1975; it is reproduced here to underline our serious concern about the gap.

Developments since 1973 have, if anything, underscored the need for constructive policies designed to increase domestic energy production. Demand has begun to rise again all over the world and protectionist and conservationist policies continue to limit export availabilities in both OPEC and non-OPEC producing countries. Furthermore, the base cost of foreign imports is fixed by the producer governments in terms of what they believe the market will bear. It seems obvious that, to the extent that the U.S. increases its energy imports, it must also accept the consequences in the form of a rapidly growing negative balance of trade.

A Time to Choose uses "scenarios" to describe its views on energy consumption levels. The first scenario is called "Historical Growth" (HG) and is used to construct a baseline from which future energy savings can be subtracted. The reason for the scenario is best expressed in the report itself: "If historical growth is to be America's future, then the first question that the government and industrial planners must ask is: 'How much energy must be provided?' "[a] *Actually, the title is a misnomer, since the "Historical Growth" scenario actually reduced energy growth substantially below historical trends, which has the effect of understating the amount of conservation necessary* to reach the lower consumption levels in the other two scenarios.

A second, lower level of consumption is portrayed in the "Technical Fix" (TF) scenario, which involves further very drastic reductions. The conclusion in the report that "Technical Fix" involves no significant change in life-style is not based upon a detailed examination of the energy consumption changes that would be required.

A third, and lowest-level scenario, "Zero Energy Growth" (ZEG), may be aptly titled in terms of the impact it would have on the individual and on total consumption, but it totally lacks suggestions for policies that would call forth the new energy sources needed to replace currently dwindling reserves.

The reductions in energy consumption to reach TF and ZEG

[a]*A Time to Choose* p. 19.

Conservation alone is not enough: the past

Some people maintain the United States should delay developing additional energy supplies. They would rely entirely on conservation to eliminate our dependence on foreign oil—a dependence that now amounts to over 37% of the nearly 17 million barrels a day of oil we Americans consume.

The past is not an infallible guide to the future, but it can often be very instructive. Let's look at what happened to oil supply and demand in the U.S. over the past 10 years.

As Chart 1 shows, consumption increased 51% from 1964 through 1974—an average of 4.2% a year. U.S. oil production, however, increased only 20% in this period. The gap between the oil we use and the oil we produce therefore widened during this decade, to more than 6 million barrels a day.

This widening of the gap took place despite the fact that oil companies' capital and exploration outlays just to find and develop oil and natural gas in this country exceeded $60 billion in the 10 years through 1974. An average of more than $17 million a day, 365 days a year, for 10 consecutive years. Even so, the gap widened.

Suppose oil companies had not made that massive effort. Suppose they had just stopped drilling and consequently had not found and proved any additional domestic reserves. Suppose they had, instead, just produced oil from the reserves that had been proved by 1964. What would have happened?

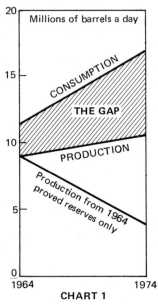

U.S. OIL
CONSUMPTION AND SUPPLY

Millions of barrels a day

CONSUMPTION

THE GAP

PRODUCTION

Production from 1964 proved reserves only

1964   1974

CHART 1

As you can see from Chart 1, U.S. oil production would have declined between 1964 and 1974. The reason is that it takes a succession of major discoveries just to maintain a country's production, much less to increase it, because once an oil field reaches its peak production, it thereafter produces at an ever-decreasing rate until it finally peters out. Compared with many fields in other countries, U.S. fields are quite old, and most of them are producing less and less oil each year. No oil field containing as much as a billion barrels has been found in the "lower 48" states of the U.S. since before World War II.

So, if no additional oil reserves had been proved up in this country between 1964 and 1974, production would have dropped by about 5 million barrels a day in that period. The gap between the oil we use and the oil we produce would have widened even further, to about 13 million barrels a day—over 75% of our total consumption.

If we had filled this gap of 13 million barrels a day with imports, the U.S. would now be running a crushing balance-of-payments drain of over $50 billion a year for oil alone. If we had tried to close the gap by drastic cuts in consumption, our economy would now probably be in far worse condition than it is.

Hard choices, those. Because when you talk about such massive cutbacks in energy supplies, you are talking about breadlines and human suffering. Very low economic growth at a time when our population is still increasing, even if at a slower rate, means a general lowering of living standards. Let nobody kid you about this.

And let nobody persuade you that conservation alone could have kept our need for oil from growing during these past ten years. Conservation alone is not enough. We must continue to develop additional supplies of energy while at the same time we work to eliminate waste in our use of it.

In the space to the right, we take a look at the United States' future need for oil in light of what the past has taught us.

Conservation alone is not enough: the future

Some of the people who would like to reduce the United States' dependence on foreign oil argue that the answer to the problem of energy supplies is to slow our country's economic growth drastically and thereby reduce our consumption of energy.

These people say we should not develop the United States' strong energy resource base until we see what a decade or more of intensive conservation can do to reduce demand. Then, they say, we can determine whether there is a need for additional supplies of energy.

We think this argument is not only specious, but dangerous.

Look at Chart 2.

As we point out in the adjoining space in commenting on the "historical" half of the chart, the 1974 gap of about 6 million barrels a day between U.S. oil consumption and production would have been about 13 million barrels a day if a no-growth domestic energy policy had prevailed from 1964 on. Or, alternatively, the U.S. would have had to slash consumption to a point that would in all probability have created enormous economic and social disorder.

What about the future? How much oil will we Americans be using by 1984, and what can we learn from the recent past?

As you can see from Chart 2, U.S. oil consumption would rise by a little over half between 1974 and 1984 if it continued to increase at the "historical growth rate" of the preceding 10 years—4.2% a year.

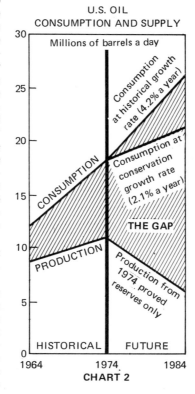

U.S. OIL
CONSUMPTION AND SUPPLY

Millions of barrels a day

THE GAP

CONSUMPTION

PRODUCTION

Consumption at historical growth rate (4.2% a year)

Consumption at conservation growth rate (2.1% a year)

Production from 1974 proved reserves only

HISTORICAL | FUTURE
1964   1974   1984
CHART 2

If this happened, our oil consumption in 1984 would be 8.5 million barrels a day higher than last year.

If, however, consumption increases only half this fast—at what might be called a "conservation growth rate" of 2.1% a year—it still will be 3.8 million barrels a day higher than it was last year. (We have discussed in earlier ads the adverse economic and social consequences of an inadequate growth rate.)

Now look at how much oil the U.S. will be able to produce in 1984 from presently proved domestic reserves

(including those on the North Slope of Alaska): just about half as much as today.

What all this tells us is that conservation alone cannot do the whole job. We must proceed to develop substantially greater domestic energy supplies. If we do not, America will be forced either to increase its already heavy dependence on oil imports or to cut energy consumption in ways that will create great economic and social turmoil.

Today about 37% of the oil we use is imported. Under even the best of circumstances, it will be difficult to reduce that percentage very much in the decade ahead.

To come anywhere near holding our own, we must continue and intensify efforts to eliminate waste in the use of energy, including the waste required by overly severe environmental restrictions. It is clear, however, that conservation alone cannot do it all.

We therefore must also proceed immediately to develop the United States' strong energy resource base. For at least the next 10 to 15 years, this means primarily conventional crude oil, natural gas, coal, and nuclear power.

The long lead times that are unavoidable in the energy industries mean we cannot delay initiating the development of additional U.S. energy supplies.

Think where we'd be if we had held off on development over the past 10 years.

would require extensive government interference in everyday life. This interference is at times expressly acknowledged; at other times, it is implied by the data in the scenarios. To the extent the assumptions on which the scenarios rest are not valid, further government involvement and controls would be required, since the recommended policies would actually prohibit development of additional energy supplies. Each layer of regulation would breed the potential for another layer; if, for example, consumers were to respond to the lower travel costs of using smaller cars by increasing the use of their cars, restrictions on travel would become mandatory in order to balance usage with available supply. *A Time to Choose* requires policies that, in effect, would restrict consumer choice, would tell people where to live, and would revamp the configuration of job opportunities. The report does not deal with other governmental policies that would be required to compensate low-income groups for the adverse effect such restrictions would have on their income.

A Time to Choose is characterized by an absence of any emphasis on supply-oriented solutions and by rejection of market forces as the means of determining usage and providing supply. Even though the U.S. has a strong resource and technology base to support development of new and existing energy sources, the use of either is rejected by the project as being unacceptable and unnecessary on the basis that curtailment in usage can solve the problem. *New supply sources must be continually found just to maintain current production and would be required even at substantially lower production levels.* Moreover, we believe the accomplishments and potential of free market forces should not be so easily dismissed.

No one denies the need for some government guidance and intervention in business affairs, and no serious businessman could argue for laissez faire treatment. For example, in the area of environmental controls, the government has intervened to set standards that would not normally be comprehended by the price mechanism. But once such standards are set, the marketplace is competent to make a proper choice within the general framework of the standard. Only if we set an *infinite* value on a particular result (such as an environmental condition) can we justify the total intervention of the government set forth in *A Time to Choose*. The pervasive regulatory framework implicit in the report would involve government deeply in areas where it has also been a demonstrable and notable failure: e.g., in stimulating the search for new energy supplies at reasonable cost to the consumer.[b] Therefore, those who suggest removing these

[b]Richard B. Mancke, *Performance of the Federal Energy Office*, (American Enterprise Institute, 1975); Stephen G. Breyer and Paul W. MacAvoy, *Energy Regulation by the Federal Power Commission* (The Brookings Institution, 1974).

decisions from the marketplace are implicitly attributing infinite values to their own conception of the "right" environmental and social factors.

There are essentially two alternatives in dealing with the energy problem. The first would delay the development of new supplies *on the assumption* that energy usage can easily be reduced enough to bring supply and demand into balance. This is the case which *A Time to Choose* implicitly adopts. The second alternative, not covered in *A Time to Choose*, would increase supplies, eliminate waste usage, and examine all implications of further energy reductions that might have an impact on life-styles. We should ask ourselves which course carries the greater risk. If the assumptions behind the low-growth cases are wrong, the result will be energy scarcity, high energy prices, unemployment, and other economic and social dislocations. On the other hand, if the assumptions supporting the case for increased supplies are wrong, we will have energy surplus and low prices. It seems clear to us that the second risk is more tolerable. In the latter case alternatives would be available; in the former, no choice would be possible.

A Time to Choose leaves the reader with an impression that the solution to all energy problems is simply to use less and that the consequences of using less are trivial. (We are sure that the residents, schoolchildren, businesses, and workers who have suffered so much during the winter months of early 1977 cannot believe that a shortage of energy is a trivial matter.) In a contrived scenario the problem of obtaining energy supplies can be made to seem of slight importance. To help the reader correlate our comments with *A Time to Choose*, the following outline is offered as a guide.

Our second section, "The Alternative to *A Time to Choose*," emphasizes the opportunities of the available base of technology and resources which, when working in tandem with realistic conservation, can provide a solution to the energy problem with the least impact on the economy and the individual.

The third section, "The Climate for Decision Making on Energy," seeks to explain why at this juncture, over four years after the start of the Energy Policy Project and over three years after the events of 1973, there is still not a national consensus on all the key elements of an energy policy. Even the energy bill enacted at the end of 1975 will make the U.S. more dependent on imports and will lead to greater regulation. This section examines the current atmosphere in which the hard decisions needed for energy policy become even harder because of the lack of a clear public understanding of energy issues and an absence of effective leadership.

Section 4 examines the conceptual framework of *A Time to Choose* which has served as the replacement for an integrated analysis of all the costs and benefits of energy. In the context of *A Time to Choose*, conservation was made a goal unto itself and loses its meaning in terms of waste, economic trade-offs, environmental significance, and individual determination. Curtailing consumption is the objective and the standard; in no sense are the costs of this balanced against the costs of increasing supplies.

"The Scenarios and the System of Analysis," in section 5, deals with the scenario chapters of *A Time to Choose* (chapters 1 through 4). It demonstrates the critical lack of a factual foundation for the project's easy "conservation" conclusion. We have already mentioned the serious shortcomings of the "Historical Growth" scenario as an extrapolation of historical growth.[c]

Employment, economic growth, and the environment are all closely related to energy supply and usage, yet the parts of *A Time to Choose* that would seem to deal with these subjects are not linked to the scenarios. Chapter 8, the environmental discussion, serves only to generate a negative image of all activities that would consume or produce energy; it is of no aid in understanding the differences in the environment of each scenario and avoids determining what the energy supplies for each should be. Chapter 5, which quantifies in terms of energy the relationship between family income and life-style, stands in isolation and remains unused in the development of the recommendations and conclusions. Chapter 6 and its related appendix F (on the role of energy in employment and economic growth) also contribute to the illusion of easy conservation; superficially, these seem to support the scenarios. In fact, a careful examination of the assumptions required to make such a superficial connection leads to an entirely different conclusion: conservation not based on rational consideration of all costs and benefits carries enormous penalties in terms of economic welfare. To provide a technical description of the special assumptions used

---

[c]Unfortunately, some defenders of *A Time to Choose* seem to have chosen not to understand the intended purpose of the "Historical Growth" scenario as it was described earlier in these comments and by the project itself. There were obviously many forecasts of future energy growth which included numbers comparable to those in the "Historical Growth" scenario, but *in every case where the assumptions were specified*, these forecasts had already assumed that actions would be taken to reduce historical growth levels in the future. In short, all responsible forecasters have reached their own conclusions as to the effect of conservation, technological improvements, and price on energy consumption. It would amount to double counting of savings to take forecasts which *include* these factors as deviations from the historical growth trends, and then to reduce the total further to reflect the same savings (in the Technical Fix and Zero Growth scenarios).

in the project's economic analysis, we have prepared appendix A.

Chapter 9 of *A Time to Choose*, "Private Enterprise and the Public Interest," employs the peculiar literary style popular today among those critical of the institutions of our society. This style seeks to create images that prevent the reader from retracing the argument to see which conclusions are valid or supported. In our Section 6, "Chapter 9 and Big Oil," we show that the very same evidence and authorities cited there can be used to arrive at another and more valid image of energy producers, one quite different from the negative image created in *A Time to Choose*.

We believe that the range of choices can be much broader than those considered in *A Time to Choose*. We believe the costs, benefits, and risks of each option must be carefully considered. We believe the national goals of full employment, individual economic growth, environmental improvement, and national security are reconcilable within a least-cost optimization of energy policy. We hope the following will help in ending the fruitless attempts to meet energy problems with easy solutions that do not require considering the real issues.

EVENTS SINCE *A TIME TO CHOOSE* WAS PUBLISHED

Many of the comments made when *A Time to Choose* was published involve matters of judgment on which reasonable people could differ, and some of the arguments we have with the project directors and with some members of the advisory board continue to fall in that category. But the passage of time has unfortunately provided confirmation of the sterility of the policies advocated by the report. In the period since the report was issued, the United States has essentially adopted the "no supplies" policy (albeit by default) with the results that:

U.S. imports have increased from 28 percent (1973) of total consumption to over 40 percent (1976);

U.S. production of crude oil has declined from nearly 10 million barrels per day to 8 million barrels per day; and,

the price of foreign oil, OPEC and non-OPEC alike, is higher now than the levels set in 1973.

While the development of new supplies has thus been neglected, the consumption of gasoline and other forms of energy (including electricity) has again begun to increase as the economy shakes off the effects of recession and economic growth resumes. There has been no lack of effort in Washington to have many of the principles of *A Time to Choose* enacted into legislation; indeed the director of the project has been personally involved in these efforts.

These efforts have prevented any consensus in the country on the best way to develop our energy resources, either conventional or exotic, but the public has not been convinced that it should accept the regimentation required by the "conservation" ethic. On the contrary, the automobile companies were induced to orient their manufacturing operations towards the smaller cars, but when true consumer participation in this decision made its impact felt, the manufacturers were left with unsold inventories of small cars and shortages of larger cars. Yet, surprisingly, some purport still to believe that the message of *A Time to Choose* is sound. It seems to us that such a conclusion must be based on an upside down value system; our only perception of the United States energy situation since 1974 is that it looks "worse and worse." And it will continue to get worse the more we curtail the development of new energy supplies by making environmental concerns the overriding objective, without regard for economic consequences.

Section 2

The Alternative to <u>A</u> <u>Time</u> <u>to</u> <u>Choose</u>

We firmly believe the safest course for the U.S. will be to encourage the development of additional energy supplies while continuing the national dialogue with respect to the desirable level of consumption—whether it be "Historical Growth" or otherwise. In all likelihood, the correct answer will not be as simple as any of the scenarios suggested; a mixed strategy will most likely be called for. We would like to suggest some elements of such a strategy.

First, government should establish a climate favorable for development of additional energy sources, in a clear and orderly way which avoids conflicting bureaucratic procedures and organizations that hinder timely and efficient production and the long-range planning which must precede it.

Second, we should go forward with the orderly development of supplies, even to the point of creating an energy surplus again. Time lost cannot be easily regained, but a development plan may be modified at any stage in its implementation; we must recognize that decisions will be made one at a time. Coal mines will be opened one at a time. Oil wells offshore will be drilled one at a time. Refineries will be built one at a time.

Third, the timetable on environmental objectives should be carefully reviewed in relation to energy needs. Here, we particularly emphasize that we refer to the *timetable* and not to objectives that result in needed improvement of the environment. We continue to believe that the advance of technology and the development of clean energy sources will permit us to realize

17

the major part of our environmental objectives. We only ask that the two programs be viewed as part of a single problem, allowing for trade-offs between them.

Fourth, we must encourage energy research so that the problems that we have experienced in the 1970s will not again become problems in the 1980s and 1990s. Energy resources are *abundant;* if we have the technology and the will to utilize them in an optimal fashion, we need have no concern for future energy growth. Coal alone can satisfy our energy requirements for centuries, and there is no reason why coal land cannot be restored and emissions from smokestacks cleaned up. There is still much oil and natural gas to be found and extracted. Beyond these, the power of the atom and the sun promise unlimited potential.

Finally, we must deal directly with the social costs of higher-priced energy. Higher energy costs will create dislocations in the economy. To the extent that there is an adverse impact on the lower-income segments of the economy, we must deal with that problem and not turn our backs on it. To deal directly with it (e.g., by subsidy) rather than through a general distortion of price levels will in the end be the most effective and least expensive solution. In overcoming hardship, it is more productive to supplement in some way purchasing power of, let us say, the disadvantaged 20 percent of society, than to distort the cost of goods and services available to the other 80 percent. Moreover, restricting energy supplies and thereby economic growth means lower absolute growth in the incomes of those least advantaged. Arbitrary controls that delay the development of additional supplies only aggravate the problem of the poor. (The history of rent controls in New York City is a prime example.)

This solution to the energy problem would involve fewer controls than *A Time to Choose* implies; would involve a return to a possible surplus of energy as a means of keeping prices down; would involve reasonable preservation of our environmental objectives; and would involve explicit attention to the problems of the poor.

The Climate for Decision Making on Energy

A Time to Choose takes advantage of a unique period of indecisiveness to place into the record a blueprint for extension of government control into many parts of American life as the advocated response to the important energy questions. The way in which the energy problem has been faced in the United States is in sharp contrast to our treatment of major crises in the past. Typically, in the past our greatest national crises have surrounded war-like situations, and the response has been characterized by a ground swell of public support for a common position. There is no such consensus on the subject of energy. There are a great many reasons for this, of which only a few will be noted here.

The first is a spreading and peculiarly schizophrenic attitude toward government. While Americans for the most part are unhappy with the way in which government departments function, there is a strong willingness on the part of many of their representatives to suppose that creating more and more governmental agencies can be ever so much more effective than those agencies that have been in existence for many years.

There are several reasons governmental agencies do not perform strictly commercial functions efficiently, but one of the important factors that condemns such ventures to failure is the American attitude toward the utilization of trained people in government. Any person whose background and experience is related to a business function in an industry that the government has or is about to regulate is shunned for employment in an agency with those regulatory responsibilities. By choice, the government is therefore shutting itself off from the most fertile source of talent available to it. Nor is this practice one which is generally accepted among governments of the Western world. The major governments of Western Europe and Japan do not hesitate to appoint qualified people from industry to government jobs in ministries having surveillance over those industries, preferring to select men of knowledge and experience while protecting the public interest by seeking to attract those with the integrity to deal honorably with the public trust. The U.S. government seems to have decided that it is too difficult to search for knowledge combined with integrity, and that initial ignorance is the best available substitute. It is not that the people selected are deficient, but rather that it takes a long time to reach the point on the learning curve where they can be productive and constructive on complex subjects. At that time, many of them choose to leave government. The result can only be indecisiveness, delay, and mistakes— while the energy problem worsens.

The failure to see the potential for a real consensus in the country has provided a fertile ground for exploitation by a multitude of politicians. The lack of a majority for any national policy within the Congress makes it easy indeed for a member to be irresponsible and to hawk cheap platitudes for political advantage, in the knowledge that the position he takes has little chance of being enacted but has the chance of garnering a few votes among those who may think he serves the public interest.

Nor have the electronic and print media dealt with the problem in a way designed to produce a coherent national policy. Television, whose few news programs are in fact judged by their entertainment value, is ill equipped to deal with an energy problem which in its complexity is intellectually demanding. As a consequence, the supply aspects of petroleum during the embargo were often dealt with by television interviews with tank-truck drivers rather than with those people responsible for supply levels. While this may be entertaining to the public, it hardly contributes to a better understanding of the issues. The desire to break a story that sounded dramatic, rather than to take the time to check facts, produced such incredible stories as the one about a host of tankers waiting outside New York Harbor for the price to increase. Although no such tankers ever existed, this story commanded prime time news coverage over a number of days and even months. Similarly, stories that oil companies were withholding fuel from the United States Navy during the embargo were widely broadcast, although the Navy never supported such a story, and it was universally denied by the oil companies responsible for supply. The famous "capped wells" in the Gulf of Mexico were yet another example of a so-called news story which was run without a check on its validity. Yet when the industry was praised by the European Economic Community (the Common Market) for its operations during the embargo, the story was buried; favorable Federal Energy Administration and congressional reports get similar treatment.

A corporation cannot recover for libel as an individual could if false statements were made about him. Consequently, there is no legal incentive for newsmen to ensure that statements made about corporations are in fact true or have a reasonable likelihood of being true. It is, therefore, relatively painless for the lazy reporter to write a story in a flashy style, even though a retraction may sometimes appear (albeit deep on inside pages) some days or weeks later.

The era of the investigative reporter with the exciting story exposing one shortcoming or another in high places comes with an important cost. The mentality that fosters criticism as the only comment on a subject does not contribute to the orderly solution of problems. Indeed, such an approach only makes it more difficult for the leadership of the nation to make the hard decisions.

A fear of criticism spawns the attitudes we have seen in the Federal Energy Administration. President Ford and the head of that agency both publicly stated that their objective was to get out of the price control business. However, in normal bureaucratic fashion the FEA continued to issue even more regulations calling for burdensome reports and more and more complex strictures over pricing in the petroleum industry. And yet, paradoxically, refined petroleum products are not in short supply, nor have they been for some years; there has been adequate crude oil available in the *world* since the end of the oil embargo; there is a surplus of marine tonnage to transport this crude oil; and there is a worldwide surplus of refining capacity to make petroleum products of all sorts. The justification for price controls over petroleum products (as distinct from price controls on crude oil or natural gas), therefore, does not arise from economic considerations nor from the need of the public, but rather from a sense of insecurity on the part of the government when it faces the conceptual issue of dismantling price controls.

The current atmosphere has another feature which can be seen in the Congress today. All of us have been aware of the shortcomings of the seniority system; and, unfortunately, some leaders in the past received important posts for which they were not qualified. Yet, it is also true that senior leaders with continuity in their posts often developed uncommonly detailed knowledge of the complex areas for which they were responsible. Many of these men served the public exceedingly well as they dealt with the problems they faced over the years. Wiping out the seniority system brings fresh faces without knowledge into these posts; a few of these people will quickly learn their jobs and may well serve the public interest better than their predecessors. Most will be thrust into a new arena to serve two years or so, never acquiring an understanding of the problems before moving on to still another spot where their performance will be equally undistinguished. The pressure of work load on elected representatives in Washington today is so great and the problems so diverse that in many cases the result is to deliver control over legislative programs and key policy decisions by default to partisan staffs not elected by the people.

Ignorance of complex issues such as those involved in energy is also a source of uncertainty; and when uncertainty prevails, the response is often to tear down rather than build when a negative program has fewer critics than a positive one. Our private enterprise system is far from perfect, but it has come a long way from the days of laissez faire capitalism. The robber barons of the last century are dead now, and the companies where they once served bear little resemblance to their predecessors of fifty or more years ago. Of course not all businessmen are responsible, but on what evidence are we to evaluate claims that the caliber of the people in government are *more* responsible? Most modern businesses recognize that any long-term planning on their part must be consistent with the role of their business as a responsible citizen of the community. Yet critics on all sides assail the profit system. *They offer no better alternatives*, but their criticism is extremely corrosive on the body politic. The alternatives offered involve more and more government, without any evidence that government can begin to do the job well.

In a trillion-dollar economy, there are simply no easy ways to turn around, in the course of a few months, the mistakes of a generation of mismanagement of energy policy, but the search for quick solutions and conspiracies to explain away subjects that are more complicated than one would like them to be is all too common a response.

Quick solutions are not only impossible, but any solution at all involves our reliance on people who are not subject to our control. Thus, in the last quarter of the twentieth century we find ourselves dependent for energy supplies on our relations with foreign countries. This is a new experience to us, one which some resent bitterly. Nevertheless, Western Europe and Japan have been in this posture for many years (although, paradoxically, Western Europe is now seeing the approach of better days in energy self-sufficiency). *The*

*fact that we cannot order other sovereign nations to do our bidding
on energy matters would not come as a surprise to other governments, but it seems to come as a surprise to us.*

So it is that when the wealthiest nation in the world, with the
finest technology and the most skilled management techniques,
finds itself in the 1970s in the midst of an energy crisis, the solutions that have proved successful in meeting national crises in the
past go unutilized. Critics now challenge the profit system, so successful in the past, as inherently bad, rather than harnessing it to
the needs of the future. Instead, an atmosphere of polarization,
self-criticism and suspicion, together with not a little irresponsible
political barnstorming, continues to exacerbate the crisis rather than
to foster creation of coherent programs for solving it. Yet this
country is rich in energy resources and will continue to be so as far
ahead as we can foresee, even with continued growth in energy usage.[a]
Paradoxically, we are unable to reach a consensus on the need to
develop these resources. Projections, forecasts, and scenarios, from
whatever origin, all indicate the need to start developing new resources, or imports of energy will expand. But despite a widespread
assumption that U.S. interests dictate substantial self-sufficiency
in strategic materials, facilities, and resources, there is still no national resolve to stimulate domestic energy production.

*The contribution which A Time to Choose makes to the problem
is not inconsequential. Far from suggesting solutions, the report is
a blatant effort to substitute pervasive government controls for
many of the elements of free choice which today are in the hands
of consumers.* The development of energy supplies is dismissed in
that report out of fear that people will use energy if they can buy it.
A Time to Choose goes so far as to state: "The net effect of a highly
favorable economic climate for energy supply could amount to a

[a]As we had indicated in our dissent to the Preliminary Report of the Energy
Policy Project, and as we will again show in later pages of this document, both
we and the project recognize that the energy resources of the world are virtually unlimited if one includes geothermal, nuclear, solar, wind, and tidal
energy, etc. As for oil, the potential there is also still very large. For example,
we have not really begun to explore the continental margins. In just one such
area, the North Sea, it is evident that Norway and the United Kingdom—both
substantial importers of energy—will become self-sufficient within a few years.
The same possibility exists for a number of other nations, with obvious implications for the world oil supply. Moreover, the U.S. has enormous coal resources,
much of which can be mined on environmentally acceptable terms, and the
technology to burn it cleanly will soon be available. If coal were to be the
only energy source, it would be available for centuries—certainly enough time
for more exotic energy sources (solar, fission, etc.) to be made available. Decisions to limit our future use of energy must therefore involve considerations
other than ultimate supply.

'self-fulfilling prophecy' for energy growth."[b] Our response is: If our energy resources (including coal, nuclear, and solar) are adequate for this century, the next, and beyond, then selling energy to consumers who want it at a price which will produce new supplies not only makes good business sense but is precisely the way that our private enterprise system has operated since the beginning of our national history. We all like challenge even if it makes our jobs more difficult, *but the criticisms leveled by the EPP against the private enterprise system are not constructive.* A deeper study of the counterproductive results of such criticisms is clearly warranted.[c]

---

[b]*A Time to Choose*, p. 37.

[c]Foundations would be well advised to direct some future study towards an examination of the role which the lack of constructive leadership and the plethora of critics at the federal government level have played in creating the current energy situation. A brief listing of the counterproductive results of the lack of constructive leadership would include:

1. In 1959 the mandatory import program was installed; modifications up through 1972 progressively discouraged the growth of U.S. refining capacity.
2. The pipeline from the North Slope of Alaska was treated as a political football for more than five years while the industry marked time waiting for approval, and this delay had brought exploration in Alaska to a virtual standstill.
3. The virtual government moratorium on federal offshore leasing from 1969 through 1972 sharply reduced the amount of acreage available for exploration in the United States.
4. The suspension of operations on the leases in the Santa Barbara channel prevented exploration of leases that had already been purchased, and prevented the full development of discoveries already made. Some of the known reserves in that area are still not on production.
5. The regulation of natural gas at a price lower than its heating value created enormous demand for the use of this fuel, while at the same time reducing the incentive to search for new gas supplies.
6. The telescoping of the timetable for achieving low automotive emission levels effectively required the manufacture of automobiles with low efficiency, rather than permitting the orderly development of technology that would retain efficiency and meet the emission requirements at the same time.
7. The White House has estimated that the initial effect of the 1975 Energy Policy and Conservation Act with be to *increase* oil imports by 150,000 barrels per day.

The Conceptual Framework of the Report

It is important to understand the differences in philosophical perspective from which we approach the functioning of the American economic system as compared with the viewpoint of *A Time to Choose*. *There extends through the entire report a pervasive—indeed almost ideological—distrust of the private economy and an equal predisposition toward government intervention.* Unless this overriding viewpoint is perceived by the reader, the hidden implications of this report (and its ultimate impact on American life) may go unrecognized.

A disdain for the free enterprise economy as it functions today is evident; the report is replete with references to public distrust of private corporations, particularly oil companies. Its suggestions comprise a blueprint for the extension of government control into many parts of American life. They include: government action to mandate uneconomic decisions regarding energy use in the various sectors; a restructuring of the job market toward low-productivity government-service occupations; mandated standards for the size, configuration, and location of homes; and various proposals for the establishment of an extensive governmental role in the energy industry—including a U.S. federal corporation for oil and gas development and the possible nationalization of the industry. Inconsistently, government departments having extensive experience with the energy industry are thoroughly criticized because they are "not capable of addressing the crucial policy issues."

In sum, the ideological bias of this report is clearly framed. It distrusts private development and favors government development.

The report's recommendations would have profound impact on America's way of life; in considering it, every American must answer fundamental ideological questions regarding the future of private enterprise and concomitantly, the dangers of burgeoning government controls on life-styles. Focusing on a second concept, the study displays a peculiar ambivalence toward technological development as a means of solving energy problems. While *A Time to Choose* proposes technological advances in order to meet its "conservation" goals through reduced energy growth, it is unwilling to consider the contributions modern technology can make on the supply side. The same technological genius that can develop and install technology to reduce energy consumption can develop energy supplies that are readily accessible, environmentally sound, and compatible with the long-run resource base (which itself can obviously be enlarged by technological advances).

Let it be clear, we hold no bias against conservation. Instead, we believe: first, obvious waste must be eliminated; second, energy use will be reduced automatically in instances where that is a rational economic decision; third, all the costs must be recognized, including the cost of government-mandated conservation and the cost of shortages that could have been avoided. This, however, is not the way in which the concept of conservation is used in *A Time to Choose.* There, EPP has exaggerated the quantification, confused waste with rational economic selection, replaced choice with mandates, and has consistently failed to provide an understandable estimate of the costs. EPP's biased view of conservation is not limited to an understatement of the positive effects of technology upon energy production. It is also characterized by a "psychology of fear" with regard to the effects of energy production on the environment. This attitude is clearly evident in chapter 8, "Energy and the Environment." Allusions are made to the true facts, but these are overshadowed by the negative tone of the prose. An example is the treatment of coal mining on pages 182–187. The major problems of underground mining are noted, such as the safety hazards and the black lung disease. It is also noted albeit with less emphasis, that some mines (those owned by steel companies) have an accident rate that is low for any occupation, and that the Federal Coal Mine and Safety Act of 1969 will go a long way toward rectifying the problem of black lung. Clearly then, the report documents a potential for solving these major problems. One must then wonder why the report is so negative on prospects for greater coal production. A similar opposition of stated fact to assumed conclusion can be seen with regard to Western coal. *A Time to Choose* used an authoritative source to support its contentions that *some* major arid Western areas are difficult to reclaim after coal mining, but then totally failed to emphasize that the same source provides the information that areas *suitable* for economic reclamation involve vast tonnage of low-sulphur coal.

Nor are these the only inconsistencies in chapter 8. Page 189 states that recent positive effects of cleanup and air quality may be reversed if there is a substantial shift to the use of high-sulphur coal in urban power plants. Depending on time of year and local climate even this would *not necessarily* always result in a harmful degradation of air quality. However, the chapter also notes that the cost of controlling air pollution from high-sulphur coal would add no more than 10 percent to the price of electricity, and that major new coal supplies will come from the low-sulphur reserves of coal in the West. If then there is safe, clean coal available and if emissions from "dirty" coal can be adequately cleaned at a low price, *why is the project so preoccupied with the thought that coal production must be severely curtailed?* This is another example of not letting facts get in the way of a preset objective. Environmental problems should not be treated lightly, but a course of least risk can be developed, one which is compatible with the energy consumption essential to our society.

The chapter on the environment thus is not a constructive attempt to find the optimum practical route toward environmental protection. Chapter 8 simply catalogues allegations of all types as to the negative effect of energy on the environment.

Use of this psychology of fear reaches a climax in the section entitled "Global Limits to Energy Use" where the reader is informed that some scientists predict a radical cooling of the earth as the result of carbon dioxide buildup, while others point to an exactly opposite effect. Obviously, both cannot occur, yet the project treats each allegation uncritically.

While the risks of energy production are overstated, any concurrent benefits of such production and use are ignored by chapter 8. Almost every activity carries with it certain inherent risks, but the decision whether to undertake such risks can only be made by measuring the risk against the incremental benefit of the activity. Chapter 8, however, forsakes such an analysis for a diatribe highlighting only negative effects that might be associated with any energy source of practical importance in the next twenty to twenty-five years.

The subject matter of *A Time to Choose* and almost every one of EPP's individual consultant reports—twenty volumes have been published so far—deal with highly controversial subject matter. They touch the very heart of the American life-style, American business, and America's relationship to the rest of the world. *Supplementary views and criticisms by scholars and experts not associated with EPP were to have been appended in the publication of each of the individual subject reports. This plan, however good in theory, was not implemented.* The majority of the volumes (twelve of the twenty published) do not contain any reviews, even the most controversial; among these is "Energy and Agriculture in the Third World," a report which portrays the Communist People's Republic of China as the epitome of success among third world nations. Surely, scholars and experts who value individual choice more highly than centralized suppression of individual freedom could have been found to balance that publication.

The EPP's contrived view of "conservation" is perhaps most clearly evidenced by the statement in *A Time to Choose* that "the net effect of a highly favorable economic climate for energy supply could amount to a self-fulfilling prophecy for energy growth." This is a transparent attempt to divert attention from thoughts of using the tools of technology, government, and diplomacy to obtain low-cost, secure, and environmentally safe energy supplies; and it must raise questions of motivation. Are we dealing with a political methodology for attempting to create artificially a common ground among environmentalists, chauvinists, and disadvantaged economic groups? If the latter is the case, the effort is doomed to failure. All but the most extreme environmentalists should recognize that technology will make a major contribution to improving conditions. Chauvinists should recognize that national weakness must result from stunted economic growth. The leadership of the less advantaged groups in our society has already recognized that the optimum route to their advancement is via economic growth and that they are the most burdened by excessively high energy costs, no matter how benevolent government is in trying to redistribute the burden. Thus, the abhorrence of adequate energy supplies at attractive cost displayed by *A Time to Choose* is counter to the interests of the very groups from which it most often seems to be trying to enlist support.

From our earliest involvement and throughout our association with the project as an advisor, we urged that it deal strictly with energy. Indeed we begged for it to avoid recriminations and political philosophy. Unfortunately, our efforts were to no avail. We continually attempted to show that suppressing the development of energy supply and failing to make provision for new sources would do the greatest disservice to those in our country having less than average access to the goods and services of our society. We attempted to show how efforts that created artifically low prices in the short run would increase energy costs in the long run. Despite our efforts, the final report of the EPP makes no provision for new energy sources and creates an atmosphere conducive to counterproductive restrictions upon energy producers which will hinder the development of energy supply for the future. Despite our efforts, the final report of the EPP has a tone of recrimination and accusatory innuendo which remains unreconciled with its tone of concern for the least advantaged people.

A Time to Choose is significantly subtitled "America's Energy Future" and thereby would be expected to focus upon the available consumption and supply options, as well as the relationship of these to the nation's economy, environment, and the implications for the citizens of this country. It is quickly apparent that the study does not live up to this promise. The study, by use of scenarios in the first four chapters, presents somewhat quantified illustrations of the feasibility and implications of some of the energy options, but there is a failure to focus on the meaning of the scenarios for the average citizen in terms of the goods and services available to him and, indeed, in terms of his way of life. Moreover, beyond the first four chapters, even this limited cohesion disappears; many of the remaining chapters of A Time to Choose are simply free-standing essays.

Chapter 5, for instance, reports the results of a survey to de-determine the relationship between consumer income and energy consumption, but this valuable information is not integrated into the remainder of the report; there is no effort to apply the survey results to the future income levels in the scenarios.

Similar problems are present in the remaining chapters. Even the critical section on reconciling energy needs and environmental goals stands apart from the rest of the text. Here the report finds that energy consumption and production almost invariably carry an environmental cost, but it always deals in absolutes, never weighing the cost of alternatives to energy consumption. It shuns any effort to select the energy sources which would cause the least environmental damage, although we repeatedly urged them to do so.

The greatest deficiency of A Time to Choose is its failure to really choose. The report realizes the immense energy resource potential of the United States but avoids discussing any constructive policies to convert those resources into usable energy (table 4-1). The report emphasizes the environmental problems associated with supplying and using those resources but avoids constructive recommendations as to which resource is the least troublesome environmentally.

Instead, the report promotes the mistaken notion that conservation policies would eliminate the need for such a hard choice; yet, even if one is willing to accept EPP's most distorted view of energy requirements ("Zero Energy Growth"), 13 quadrillion BTUs more energy are consumed in 1985 than in 1973 and 25 quadrillion BTUs more energy are required by 2000. In addition to this growth in energy, the energy sources being used up also must be replaced. In the course of time the production from each oil well declines and coal mines reach the end of their seams. The decline in production from existing sources must be added to the growth in energy requirements for 1985 and 2000.

While we object strongly to the way in which the hard choices on energy are hidden in *A Time to Choose*, we do not object to the elimination of waste, we do not object to reductions in energy consumption resulting from individual economic decisions, and we do not object to energy reductions resulting from national decisions when based on improving the collective welfare of individuals. But *A Time to Choose* goes far beyond these useful types of conservation when it recommends mandating reduced energy use, without regard to the cost in terms of individual welfare. Moreover, even in the "Technical Fix" scenario, it is recognized that many of the reductions in usage would have a one time only effect, after which energy usage would continue to resume its growth. How and under what conditions would the required supplies become available? The answer is not to be found in *A Time to Choose*.

Table 4-1. Major U.S. Energy Resources (Years of Life at 1973 Rate of Total Energy Consumption) (For definitions see *A Time to Choose*, p. 26)

	Reserves	*Additional Recoverable Resources*	*Remaining Resource Base*
Petroleum	5–7	15–30	200
Natural Gas	6–8	15–30	97
Oil Shale	12–45	100	2000
Uranium			
Thermal reactors	3	8	107
Breeder reactors	290	590	7500
Coal	67	(Unspecified)	1040

Section 5

The Scenarios and the System of Analysis

A Time to Choose centers on a discussion of three scenarios. The cornerstone scenario is "Historical Growth"; the others are supposedly derived from it by adjustments described in the report. The "Historical Growth" (HG) case involves the highest consumption levels; a case is then constructed at a somewhat lower growth level, and this case is called "Technical Fix" (TF), a term that brings to the reader's mind the image of relatively easy "adjustments" to a functioning system. Finally, there is a scenario called "Zero Energy Growth" (ZEG) that is intended to bring the energy consumption pattern to *a level state by 2000*. Both of the two lower cases represent variations on the "Historical Growth" case, and much of the work in the report involves a discussion of differentials in relation to "Historical Growth." None of these scenarios is offered as a forecast, although the reader can clearly understand the author's preference for scenarios involving reduced or zero growth in energy consumption.

In short, EPP's offering is sequential: a scenario is constructed which is represented as the state in which we now find ourselves; some relatively minor adjustments reduce growth to an intermediate slope, and a further step takes us down to an eventual plateau in energy use.

"HISTORICAL GROWTH"

Since so much of the presentation rests upon the concept that the "Historical Growth" scenario is a realistic simulation of current energy consumption, it is important to examine that concept at the outset. "Historical Growth" purports to be a simulation based on the average conditions of the 1950–70 period, extrapolated to produce a 1985 requirement of 116 quadrillion BTUs.

To be sure, any of a number of detailed energy studies by respected authorities could have served as a strategy point to construct an "Historical Growth" base case. Table 5-1 summarizes ten forecasts by a group of established experts of quite diverse backgrounds and interests. In addition to the sources listed in the table, a study prepared by the Brookhaven National Laboratory for the Office of Science and Technology in 1972 projected 1985 consumption at 117 quadrillion BTUs and a report by the Department of Interior later in the same year made the same projection; both studies comprehended higher energy prices and other discontinuities in energy relationships.

It should first be emphasized that, apart from the EPP scenarios, the other authorities cited in the table intended their figures to represent *forecasts*, not the continuation of historical trends. (Nevertheless, the "Historical Growth" scenario is the lowest projection on the table, with all the others equaling or exceeding 120 Q BTUs.)

Table 5-1. Available Projections of Energy Requirements

Source and Publication Date	1985 Quadrillion BTU	1985 Percent Increase Over 1973	Difference vs. EPP-HG Quadrillion BTU[i]
EBASCO Services Inc. (1970)	120	60	+4
Federal Power Commission (1971)	124	65	+8
Department of Interior (1971)	128	71	+12
Petroleum Industry Research Foundation (1971)	129	72	+13
Ford, Bacon and Davis Inc.-Engineers (1971)	152	103	+36
Stanford Research Institute (1972)	143	91	+27
Institute of Gas Technology (1972)	125	67	+9
National Petroleum Council (1972)	125	67	+9
Council on Environmental Quality (1973)	124	65	+8
Atomic Energy Commission (1973)	121	61	+5
EPP's "Historical Growth" (1974)	116	55	—
Memo: EPP's "Technical Fix" (1974)	92	23	-24
EPP's "Zero Growth" (1974)	88	17	-28

[i]Four quadrillion BTU is the equivalent of the reduction in the rate of flow of oil supplies to the U.S. during the worst of the 1973–74 embargo; 8 quadrillion BTU is equal to the energy consumed by all passenger cars in 1970; 12 quadrillion BTU is equivalent to the energy value of all coal produced in the U.S. in 1970.

Those who make forecasts of energy requirements do take account of the changes which are occurring in the rate of energy consumption and do reflect the effects of conservation, expected price changes, and technology in reducing the rate of energy consumption. Unfortunately, the assumptions regarding these factors are not always explicitly stated by those who prepare the forecast. Therefore, for the purpose of this discussion the studies by the National Petroleum Council (NPC) have been selected, because the underlying assumptions made for those studies are more extensively documented than for the others in the table.

The National Petroleum Council forecast was based on a detailed investigation of both energy supply and demand trends; it concluded that the most likely demand for 1985 would be 125 Q BTU. Since our purpose is to investigate future changes that could occur in energy demand and to see how feasible those changes are, we have to eliminate these changes from the base forecast. Fortunately, it is possible to make such adjustments for most of the important elements in the NPC forecast, as follows:

1. The NPC assumed that there would be modifications in automobile design and weight which would have the effect of reducing 1985 gasoline consumption by the equivalent of 3.8 Q BTUs.
2. It was assumed that improved insulation of houses and the construction of smaller homes would reduce 1985 residential consumption by 1.9 Q BTUs.
3. A reduction in the energy cost of generating electricity was assumed by the NPC to save in 1985 a total of 2.2 Q BTUs; when allocated by final electric consumption about 1.0 Q BTUs would be in the industrial sector and 1.2 Q BTUs in residential and commercial.
4. The NPC committee made the hopeful assumptions that "acceleration in technological development and energy conservation would be sufficient to offset energy used for environmental improvement and a greater proportionate use of electric power." This new technology and conservation was not a part of the historical scene, and if it were not available, consumption would be higher; thus, usage would increase for 1985 in electrical generation, industrial plants, and waste disposal by the significant amount of 10.2 Q BTUs.[a] Other

[a]Many argue that the additional energy requirements associated with pollution control measures can be reduced or eliminated by technology: we agree, but emphasize the considerable amount of time necessary to develop such technology. One of the reports commissioned by the EPP suggested that pollution control could actually amount to an energy credit, a position we would consider untenable, as it would require all solid waste to be used as fuel and that farm crop residue also be utilized for fuel; the latter requirement would presumably necessitate the replacement of nutrients and humus thereby removed from the land.

efficiencies necessary to offset the greater share that electrical energy would have of the total energy market would involve an additional 3.2 Q BTUs.

5. Adjustment of the NPC projection downward is required because EPP assumes a smaller population growth and replaces the robust economy that NPC envisioned with a more subdued economic growth. The NPC explicitly studied the sensitivity to each of these parameters; they would reduce energy consumption by 13.2 Q BTUs.

The net result of these upward and downward adjustments is an energy demand of 133 Q BTUs for 1985, assuming continuation of historic trends, insofar as we can identify and project them.

Table 5-2 provides the details of these adjustments and shows how each major use of energy is affected. The net result of totaling these positive and negative adjustments is compared to the "Historic Growth" of *A Time to Choose* on the final two lines of the table. Thus, it can be seen that the base from which EPP starts all energy usage analysis is 17 quadrillion BTUs below true historical growth levels.

It should be emphasized that *the resulting 1985 consumption total of 133 Q BTUs is not a forecast that the NPC or any other responsible group necessarily would endorse for the year 1985.* It is rather an extension of 1972 trends in energy consumption to reflect the 1985 economic and population levels assumed by EPP. This total establishes a baseline from which savings can be deducted to arrive at a reasonable consumption level, reflecting the introduction of new technology and conservation. *It is important to emphasize that the "Historical Growth" case of the Energy Policy Project consumes only 87 percent of the energy required under true historical growth assumptions.*[b]

---

[b]There is further evidence within *A Time to Choose* itself that the Historical Growth scenario did not represent current trends of energy consumption. The Washington Center for Metropolitan Studies report on the relationship of direct energy consumption to income is included in chapter 5. Escalating the real incomes of the poor and lower-middle groups to the median level or escalating the income levels of all income groups at the average rates used in chapter 6 produces an energy requirement of at least 125 Q BTUs in 1985. Furthermore, the calculation implies growing efficiency in energy consumption; chapter 5 notes, for instance, the higher the income of a family, the more likely it is to live in a house that is insulated and has storm windows. Clearly, most Americans want a bigger home, more appliances, and more travel if they can afford it, and clearly in the past when the economy grew they could afford more, and they got it. Americans are mobile and they want to be able to determine where they live and where they travel limited only by what they feel they can afford. Unfortunately, the contribution to understanding energy consumption made by the Washington Center for Metropolitan Studies (chapter 5) has not been integrated into the rest of *A Time to Choose.*

Table 5-2. Adjustment of 1985 National Petroleum Council Energy Projections to an EPP Frame of Reference: Quadrillion BTU

	CONSUMING SECTORS[i]			
	Residential and Commercial	*Industrial and Raw Materials*	*Transportation*	*Total*
NPC "Intermediate Case"	43.2	53.1	28.6	124.9
Non-Historical Assumptions Used By NPC[ii, iii]				
— Auto weight and design	—	—	3.8	3.8
— New insulation and smaller homes	1.9	—	—	1.9
— More efficient electric generation	1.2	1.0	—	2.2
— Additional efficiency and conservation to offset energy cost: environmental improvement in electric and industrial plants; and waste disposal	1.4	8.8	—	10.2
— Other efficiencies to offset greater relative share of electricity in final consumption	1.8	1.4	—	3.2
Adjustment to EPP Economy[ii, iv]				
— Slower Population Growth	(0.6)	(1.0)	(0.5)	(2.1)
— Slower Economic Growth	(3.7)	(5.7)	(1.7)	(11.1)
TOTAL (i.e., Historic Growth EPP Basis)	45.2	57.6	30.2	133.0
Memo: EPP "Historic Growth"	38.0	52.1	26.0	116.1
Difference	(7.2)	(5.5)	(4.2)	(16.9)
Percent EPP Below Adjusted NPC	16.0	9.5	13.9	12.7

[i]Energy costs of producing electricity has been allocated to end-use sectors.

[ii]As identified by the National Petroleum Council in *U.S. Energy Outlook*, 1973.

[iii]These reduced the NPC projection; therefore, the energy has to be reincluded.

[iv]Since NPC has faster economic and population growth these figures have to be subtracted to be consistent with EPP's framework.

Naturally, if the "Historical Growth" trend is understated, the other scenarios constructed from it will also be understated. In essence, therefore, *A Time to Choose* vastly overstates the ease with which consumption can be reduced in the "Technical Fix" and "Zero Growth" cases because the Historical Growth scenario already comprehends many of the energy-saving assumptions later relied upon to produce "Technical Fix" levels of consumption.

INFORMATION PUBLISHED SINCE
A TIME TO CHOOSE APPEARED

We communicated frequently with members of the staff during the lifetime of the project but were unable to confirm key factual underpinnings for the scenario's statistics. Since *A Time to Choose* was published, additional information has appeared, which does not alter our conclusions that: (a) the "Historical Scenario" represents a gross underestimate of energy trends as they existed in the early 1970s; (b) there is inadequate quantitative support to document the estimated effect of conservation programs; and therefore, (c) the project's policies would result in a stifling of economic growth and a lessening of individual opportunity and choice.

In contrasting our criticism of the scenarios with more recently published information, the reader, in most instances, will have to judge for himself the relative merits of our arguments; we cannot, of course, again go into detail on every item. On the other hand, there is considerable agreement with the faults we have found with the quantification in *A Time to Choose:*

1. The projection of occupied housing units was too low, thereby understating energy requirements.
2. Highly efficient small automobiles might provide incentive for Americans to drive more miles and use more gasoline.
3. The actual use of electrical heat in industrial processing was, in the early 1970s, badly overstated, thereby inflating growth projections for this use of energy.[c]
4. The energy cost of producing aluminum to reduce automobile weight was not comprehended in the scenarios.
5. The regulatory and physical infrastructure for industrial cogeneration of electricity will not be readily available and utilities will have to provide back-up capacity.

[c]Also, by the early 1970s, it was already clear that the once prevalent hopes for extremely inexpensive nuclear electricity were shattered by the costs and delays of meeting environmental requirements and by the disproportionate inflation of construction costs of nuclear plants.

6. Changes in building codes which would cost an average $1200 per household, could represent a barrier to homeownership for many lower-income families.
7. The projected growth of rail haulage is unrealistic.

A frequently cited source is *The Project Independence Report*, which was published in November 1974 and therefore could not be used by the Energy Policy Project. Moreover, *The Project Independence Report* used a very explicit price relationship as a basis for analysis, while *A Time to Choose* makes only one passing reference to price in the entire volume. Furthermore, it must be noted that the Project Independence analysts, working in the midst of the crisis atmosphere of the embargo and immediate postembargo period, comprehended many departures from historical trends in their analysis, such as 55 mph speed limits and lowered thermostats.

"TECHNICAL FIX"

The energy savings that accrue to the various technologies studied in the "Technical Fix" are, according to *A Time to Choose* (page 47), "economically justified at existing prices." But the fact is that implementation of many of these technologies requires not only the incentive of higher prices in the free market but also substantial uneconomic forced energy "savings" which are dictated by an extensive network of government mandates.

Moreover, it is characteristic of the report that public participation in energy decisions is given considerable lip service. *On page 340 it is stated that "... citizen participation is essential." Yet the report is a blueprint reducing the number of choices the average citizen may make regarding fundamental aspects of his life-style.* He would have less choice in selection of living accommodations, less choice of how and how much he travels, less choice of jobs, and less choice of how he spends the income from his labors.

In the residential sector, the bulk of the purported savings requires extensive revision of building codes throughout the United States. This revision would ignore local and regional economic incentives in the residential sector and would place on all citizens *the burden of higher initial construction costs. A Time to Choose* would raise the cost of homes by $122 billion.[d] This would work

---

[d]*A Time to Choose.* p. 470. If this figure is divided by the number of households it would yield an average of $1200, but the figure would likely be higher for private home ownership and lower for appartment construction.

extreme hardships on citizens in lower income brackets, where frequently the size of the down payment and the monthly mortgage payments determine whether or not a family can own its own home. EPP apparently did not seriously examine this implication of its recommendations, although elsewhere in the report concern over the effect of energy costs on the poor is stressed. The report justifies the need for federal government intervention to mandate installation of storm windows and insulation, first by exaggerating the benefits[e] and then by ignoring the fact that the thousands of local jurisdictions which set building codes do respond to local conditions of climate, income of their constituents, labor market operations, and the kind of housing being built (summer homes, year-round dwellings, garden apartments, high-rise, etc.). Similarly, 80 percent of the savings in the transportation sector do not result from economically viable technological advances, but from government-mandated mileage specifications for automobiles. Under the conditions presented by the EPP, one would be unable to drive a larger, safer automobile if he wished. This is so even though the larger car may be driven fewer miles (because of the cost) and might, at the end of the day, actually consume less gasoline than a smaller, lighter car that is driven many more miles. Indeed, excessively stringent, mandated mileage standards might well be counterproductive (interfering with both conservation and environmental improvement). On the one hand, the consumer might decide to keep his old, usually-more-polluting car longer if the cost, size, and performance of the new car did not satisfy him. On the other hand, the motorist might find his new lightweight car costs less per mile to run and might, therefore, drive more miles.

Aside from the obvious inconsistencies in the analysis, the report is also characterized by a lack of documentation for crucial assumptions. For example, in the industrial sector 40 percent of the reductions accruing to the TF occur in three "miscellaneous" categories.[f] In the residential sector, the quantification of savings due to insulation in homes, a fundamental savings method, was based on virtually no significant data: field surveys were not attempted,[g] and hard

---

[e]Ibid., p. 48, exaggerates the fuel savings and is inconsistent with appendix A, p. 434. The fuel savings implied on p. 48 approaches 50 percent, while on p. 434 it is assumed that the difference in heat loss between a HG and a TF house built in the 1975–85 period would be 20 percent.

[f]*A Time to Choose*, p. 465: "Miscellaneous co-generation" saves 0.4 Q BTU; "Belt Tightening" 2.0 Q BTU; "Heat recuperation with direct use of fuels" 2.9 Q BTU. (The use of electric heat in industrial processing will be discussed in more detail in later paragraphs.)

[g]*A Time to Choose*, p. 433; also p. 432 notes the lack of statistically significant field measurements on heating system efficiencies.

facts were replaced by subjective judgments (to the effect that current practice is to install two or three inches of insulation, that storm windows "sometimes" are fitted by the owner, and that initial window installation is "usually plain"). In the transportation sector, clearly overstated and undocumented measures for achieving fuel economies are presented, with only the most generalized estimates of fuel economy improvements.

The "Technical Fix" scenario represents 91.6 Q BTU consumption in 1985. Such an energy level is possible, not by "Technical Fix", but by "Fewer Consumer Choices."

"ZERO ENERGY GROWTH"

As with the "TF" scenario, the true nature of the savings in the "ZEG" scenario is nebulous. For example, in the residential sector, there is a saving resulting from reduced use of "presently unknown appliances;" the saving is 0.7 Q BTUs in 1985 and 1.6 Q BTUs in the year 2000. Surprising as it may sound, there is no further documentation or explanation given for these energy savings.

Achieving the "TF" and the "ZEG" low levels of energy usage would require extensive government interference in everyday life. People would, in effect, be told where to live; the entire configuration of the job market would be revamped; additional governmental policies would have to be implemented to compensate low-income groups for the adverse effect of ZEG on their income, and the government would have to expand in many new directions (financed by higher taxes).

Chapter 3, "Technical Fix" (TF), and chapter 4, "Zero Energy Growth" (ZEG), display the project's conjectures as to how and where energy consumption can be reduced. The claim is made for Technical Fix that energy consumption growth can be cut by large amounts "without seriously affecting improvement in the standard of living;" and the ZEG case, which eventually halts energy growth, includes the claim "this doesn't mean that people would lack the valued material amenities of the higher energy growth scenario." Yet these crucial statements are not supported by documentation.

There are no easy solutions to the problem of ensuring that the nation has enough energy. It cannot be assumed that the energy dilemma can be avoided by effortless conservation or even by inexpensive new resources and technologies. To make such assumptions only compounds the difficulties of resolving the problem by creating delay and thereby increasing the costs in future years. A careful examination of the nation's growing energy needs and the opportunities to reduce these trends would reveal the options, the difficulties, and the costs.

COMMENTS BY CONSUMING SECTOR

Residential and Commercial Sectors

Although the "Historical Growth" scenario uses a consumption level for this sector of 38.0 Q BTUs in 1985 (versus 45.2, which we have previously calculated as representing historical growth trends in existence in the early 1970s), the EPP forecast has some components that are very substantially in *excess* of historical growth trends. One of these is electric space heat, which is an area of saving where the "Technical Fix" scenario identifies an opportunity to reduce energy consumption. The project staff began with an estimate of 1970 space heating consumption which is two and a half times the best estimate of respected authorities in the field. They then projected an increase in electrically heated homes equivalent to nearly *two-thirds* of all new construction in the 1975–85 decade; this growth in units, coupled with assumed very high unit consumption, produced residential space heating requirements of 3.6 Q BTUs— or more than 1.0 Q above the comparable NPC forecast.[h] Beginning

[h]Trends existing in the early 1970s pointed to a very limited geographic area where demand for electrically heated homes was growing rapidly. (*The 1970 Census of Housing* indicates that 78 percent were in the South and West Divisions of the U.S.) It is true that electric power costs had been declining at 2 to 3 percent per year (in large part because the price of oil was also declining in real terms), but electric heat was and would continue to be the most expensive fuel in all areas of the U.S. Thus, a trends-continue case would have precluded electric space heating from making any significant penetration in the less temperate parts of this country where the bulk of the population resides and where heating costs are a significant part of a family's annual budget.

Because of the geographic limitations, it is inconceivable that the annual heat requirements for electrically heated homes would approach the average for all homes in the U.S. Yet, on page 433 of *A Time to Choose*, it is stated: "The average winter climate is about 5,000 degree days giving an annual heat loss of 70–75 million BTU's per housing unit per year," and later on the same page, "For a house with electric resistance heat, the electricity requirements would be 70–75 million BTU's. . . ." Thus, in *A Time to Choose* electrically heated homes are clearly assumed to have the same heat requirements as those using other fuels, despite the fact that most electric heat is found in the milder climates of the South and West. The average consumption of 70–75 million BTUs is equivalent to 20,000–22,000 KWH per house a total sharply at variance with a sample survey entitled *All Electrical Homes—1970* (FPC, June 1972), showing electrical consumption for heating in various parts of the country. For example: (1) Florida Power & Light Company with 390,000 customers using electric heating averaged 1000 KWH per house; (2) Southern California Edison Company with this assumed extraordinary growth for electrically heated homes, the report could then postulate very substantial savings in electrical space heating: in short, the saving in this particular area arises largely from consumption that could not arise under Historical Growth conditions.

A Time to Choose fails to distinguish between occupied houses and total housing units, a matter of some significance, since electric resistance heat in northern parts of the U.S. is largely confined to seasonal units; electric-resistance heat and heat pumps in year-round dwellings have found a market most in the more southern states—for good economic reasons.[i] Accordingly, the application of an *average* annual heat-loss figure to *all* forms of heating systems is grossly misleading since the need for heat in Florida (one of the largest markets for electric heat) is obviously less than in Maine (where oil heat has the largest market share).

After erecting this fictitious usage, EPP then proceeds to effect "savings" by converting those residences from electric heaters to heat pumps or gas and oil furnaces. Since it takes more than 3 BTUs of energy input to generate and deliver the equivalent of 1 BTU as electricity, the savings in switching to fossil fuels and heat pumps are considerable.

The space heating of commercial areas consumes the most energy in that sector, and this is also the area where the report achieves essentially all its savings. After correctly stating that very little or no electric resistance heat is used in commercial areas, the report then proceeds to concoct an unrealistically high growth scenario for resistance heat, similar to the assumptions for the residential sector. According to *A Time to Choose*, two-thirds of all commercial space built between 1975–85 would have *electric resistance* heat in the

---

with 27,000 such customers averaged 4100 KWH per house; (3) Duke Power Company (serving North and South Carolina) with 63,000 such customers averaging 10,400 KWH per house; (4) Georgia Power with 39,000 such customers averaged 11,000 KWH per home.

To further clarify the issue of home heating requirements, it may be helpful to look at the needs of several representative cities, bearing in mind two considerations; first, the project's calculation that the average U.S. winter climate is 5000 degree days (degree days are a measure of the need for heating) and second, the preponderance of electrically heated homes are in the South and West. As examples: the 1970 actual degree days recorded in New York City were 5021; Washington, D.C., 4302; Atlanta, 3023; San Francisco, 2446; Los Angeles 1188; and Miami 259.

[i] *A Time to Choose*, appendix A., uses a figure of 80 million occupied housing units in 1985, but the projections by government agencies and private economists, also available to the project, ranged from 84–88 million; a difference of 5–10 percent. Such differences expressed in terms of the estimates of residential energy usage are 1.1–2.2 Q BTUs.

"Historical Growth" scenario, and this trend continues through the year 2000, despite the very much higher cost of this type of heating. In "Technical Fix" and "Zero Energy Growth," savings are then easy to calculate: one simply replaces electric resistance heat; and since it requires 3 BTUs of fuel to make and deliver 1 BTU of heat via electricity, the savings are magnified.

The savings attributed to this single change (from electric resistance space heat to heat pumps and fossil fuel) amounts to 2.7 Q BTUs in 1985, or 65 percent of the total consumption forecast for this type of heat. The 2.7 Q BTU assumed savings is in all probability greater than the *total* electrical resistance heat usage in 1985.

The analysis of other energy consumption in the commercial sector is totally without documentation; there is neither an adequate set baseline ("HG") nor an explanation of the reductions for the future to achieve "TF" and "ZEG". The project did not examine current or historical data to determine the relationship between service sector employment and square footage, or between commercial area and energy consumption. Yet *A Time to Choose* assumes that growth in the area of office buildings, stores, hospitals, etc., will parallel the growth in service sector employment (as defined by the project); this means that the working conditions of those employed in the service sector will remain fixed for the thirty-year period 1970–2000, despite common knowledge that the work areas and ancillary facilities (washrooms, lunch rooms, computer rooms, etc.,) available to these employees have been improving historically. Thus, if the square feet available to each employee were to continue to grow, a proportionate increase in energy requirements would result, and all the scenarios would prove to be underestimated (unless, of course, the option of continued improvement in working conditions is forsaken).[j]

Transportation Sector

Eighty percent of the savings in the transportation sector involves automobiles. But there is no evaluation of the number of automobiles and the number of miles driven, and the minimal analysis is internally contradictory.[k]

---

[j]*The Project Independence Report* utilizes a formula that relates commercial square footage to disposable income. Inserting the disposable income forecast used by the project into this formula would produce an amount of commercial space comparable to that used by the project; however, as we have already noted, the consultant (DRI) which prepared the forecast of disposable income for the project acknowledged that it was constrained by energy supply deficiencies.

[k]For example, the upper table on p. 442, used to calculate fuel requirements in the high growth case, indicates that automobiles will be driven 1.2 trillion

Long-term trends were minimized by EPP and most of the increase in car ownership rates allowed between 1970–85 in the scenarios had already occurred by the end of 1973.[1] Compound growth rates are powerful factors, and small differences in annual rates yield dramatic results after a number of years. The number of cars would be 25 percent larger, at even the 1950–70 growth rate, than the projection adopted for Historical Growth.

In 1960, 65.3 percent of the population was of driving age, and this group expanded to 67.3 percent by 1970; the Census Bureau estimates (in its series "E" projections, used elsewhere by EPP), that 72.4 percent of the population will be in the driving age category in 1985.

Also relevant is the question of how many miles the average car is driven each year. *A Time to Choose* used a constant 10,000 miles per year, while the Federal Highway Administration shows that there was a mild uptrend of this figure during the past decade, despite the worsening fuel economy of cars. Since the Technical Fix scenario portrays a dramatic increase in automobile efficiency, the cost of automobile travel per mile would be moderated, and it would be likely that people would use their efficient cars to a greater extent than their less efficient "Historical Growth" cars, with corresponding loss of some of the savings assumed by the project.[m]

The greatest area of uncertainty in any study concerning future energy requirements for automobile transportation involves the forecast of automobile technology and design. In recent years, automobile efficiency has been penalized by various modifications designed to minimize air pollution and *maximize safety* (small cars may

miles in 1985. However, when it came to calculating fuel economy in the "Technical Fix" case, a higher figure for vehicle miles (1.4 trillion) was used. This latter figure is revealed by applying the number of vehicles on the road (*A Time to Choose* states the same number for cars on the road is used for both scenarios) to the table at the bottom on p. 442. Thus, EPP used the lower of two available estimates to calculate "Historical Growth."

[1] *A Time to Choose* shows a decline in the average number of people per car between 1970 and 1980 at a rate of 0.9 percent per year (from one car per each 2.28 persons to 1.99) and between 1970 and 2000 at 0.6 percent per year. But these rates are dramatically below rates experienced in both the recent and longer-term historical periods. Between 1950 and 1970 (the years EPP so often uses to justify the Historical Growth scenario), the number of people per car was declining at 2.4 percent per year; a similar rate prevailed between 1960–70. Furthermore, between 1970–73 this figure was 3.3 percent per year.

[m] This certainly is one of the ways the consumer may behave. If supplies were limited to the lower consumption estimate, as EPP's recommended policies would, then the issue of allocating gasoline to individuals and priority uses would have to be faced. The effect on the individual and his life-style would be profound; conditions in some areas of the country during the embargo are illustrative.

defeat this). Many of the safety requirements, designed to reduce fatalities and injury resulting from collisions, add weight to the vehicle. In addition, the consumer has opted for the vehicles providing greater convenience and comfort. The current proliferation of automobile air conditioning and power-assists contributed to the decline in miles per gallon. Considerable research is available concerning these technologies and designs, yet very little has been published concerning the changes required to improve efficiency. The very brief listing of techniques, claimed to lift efficiency to previously unexperienced levels, were not further investigated in the report. Yet the energy "saving" assumed in *A Time to Choose* to be achieved by improving gasoline mileage is the largest single conservation item (5.0 Q BTUs). The 1975 Energy Act gasoline mileage standards require that future cars be very much smaller than Americans have been accustomed to driving.[n] What the response of consumers will be is not yet clear. Certainly, there can be no objection to improving efficiency in gasoline usage, possibly in part via government mandate, but the schedule must be consistent with available technology and safety requirements; moreover, the final product must be salable to the consumer.

According to *A Time to Choose*, the energy requirements for transportation modes other than the passenger car accounted for about 48 percent of the usage in this sector in 1970. It is not feasible to review here the trends in all the other modes of moving people and freight, but the movement of people by buses and trains has been in steady decline for the last thirty years; and air and truck freight have been growing rapidly while railroad freight movements increased only slowly.

These trends have sprung not only from major government policies and programs (e.g., freight rate regulation, highway funding and construction) but were also supported by billions of everyday consumer decisions. Comfort, convenience, and safety (from accident and crime) are of significant value to the consumer, and speed is a measurable economic benefit both to the individual and business. A desire for privacy and individual independence may also be important influences in the public's decision as to how it will travel.

---

[n]The four gasoline-savings techniques catalogued on p. 59 (*A Time to Choose*) achieve a gasoline efficiency of only 19.5 miles per gallon when applied to the 12 MPG base. Even these are insufficient to reach the 22 MPG efficiency required in 1980 in order to achieve the 20 MPG fleet average used in Technical Fix for 1985. Moreover, the energy savings postulated would require that these small cars not be driven more miles in response to the lowered cost per mile. Note that the 1975 Energy Act standards are based on the EPA laboratory test method and the miles per gallon figures contained therein do not correspond to actual driver experience or to the data EPP has used.

Nor should economics be disregarded in trying to understand consumer behavior; it does cost less for a family to use its car for vacation transportation. For the economy as a whole, greater productivity results from greater speed in moving goods and people on job assignments, as long as incremental benefits exceed incremental costs. Consideration of these factors is needed in order to understand why people opt for cars and planes, to the neglect of buses and trains. An absence of such an understanding means more mandated choices and less individual choice. Similarly, understanding of the advancing technological state of the economy is necessary to appreciate that low-unit-value bulk commodities (which are so well adapted to the characteristics of railroads) are becoming less important, while more intensely manufactured higher-unit-value goods and services are becoming relatively more significant. This higher-unit-value production is more likely to be shipped in smaller lots more suitable for air and truck shipment where the benefits from greater speeds of these modes are measurable in dollars and cents.

A Time to Choose would dramatically alter these trends and would do so without full considerations of the infrastructure, economics, and regulatory environment which support the existing trends. For example, the "Technical Fix" scenario would have the railroads double the ton miles of freight carried between 1970 and 1985, and then again nearly double volume by the year 2000 while increasing the number of passenger miles on trains 80 percent between 1970 and 1985. By the year 2000 passenger traffic would be nearly 1000 percent of 1970.

The serious financial and operating difficulties of many railroads, particularly those in the most populous regions of the country, are noted almost daily in the newspapers. Deteriorating roadbed conditions, track abandonments, freight car shortages, and poorly met schedules continue to be all too common. However, *A Time to Choose* goes no further in suggesting means to revitalize railroads than recommending lower freight charges and work rule changes for railroad labor, all mandated by the federal government.

The reader is told only that the energy requirement in the high-growth case is 2900 BTUs per passenger mile and that in the "Technical Fix" scenario it would improve to 1000 BTUs per passenger mile, an efficiency improvement of 195 percent. We are not told how the saving would be achieved, *and the energy required to rebuild and expand railroads does not receive even passing mention.*

Similarly, current trends in the airline industry are changed without consideration for economic and regulatory realities. Airline energy efficiency (measured by load factor) is sharply increased; while at the same time, growth in both passenger and freight traffic is sharply curtailed. The economic incentive to shippers, who are increasingly opting to use air freight for shipping high-value goods and goods where freshness has value, is ignored even when much of this incentive arises because it reduces the shippers' inventory requirements. Larger inventories require more energy tied up in slower-moving goods; a fact of even more significance in the rail/truck trade-off.

Disregard for the trade-off between economies of time and economies of energy typifies the entire transportation sector discussion. Also, disregard of consumer behavior and consumer motivation, especially desires for comfort and convenience, is most clearly evident in the analysis of transportation. Ironically, government regulation has been the key element in structuring today's airline, trucking, and railroad industries, but it is to the same government that *A Time to Choose* looks to improve the transportation environment for the future; the dissatisfaction with today's government-created transportation structure only leads to a recommendation for greater government involvement.

Industrial Sector

One-half of the reduction in over-all energy consumption between the "Historical Growth" and "Technical Fix" scenarios is found in the industrial sector, and two-thirds of the additional reduction to reach "Zero Energy Growth" also occurs in this group of end-users. Unfortunately, the assumed savings in this sector rests heavily on two extremely vulnerable premises. The first is the assumption—which is contrary to findings by one of the consultants to the project—that businessmen would not act to take advantage of available energy savings. The second area of vulnerability is the arbitrary generalization of expected energy savings over large segments of industry.

As to the first point, *A Time to Choose* notes "industrial managers have been as oblivious to the opportunities for savings as have homeowners" (p. 63). All costs reduce profits; to suggest that a cost of "only about 5%" is insignificant ignores the fact that profits after tax are also only about 5 percent of the total costs which make up the price of manufactured goods; and thus, that the cost of energy in manufacturing is similar in size to the total after-tax profits in manufacturing. *To suggest that businessmen would, or do, ignore such a significant area of expense is nonsense.* Indeed, "Principal Finding Number One" in the Conference Board–National Science Foundation report to EPP[o] was: "Significant savings in energy use

---

[o]*Energy Consumption in Manufacturing*, p. 2. (One of the EPP selected reports published by Ballinger, Inc.)

have been realized by the manufacturing sector in the past. Energy use per unit of product declined at a 1.6% average annual rate from 1954 to 1967. As a result, while total manufacturing output rose 87%, total energy use rose only 53%. This was achieved in a period of stable or declining relative prices of energy.''

In regard to the second major failing in the project's analysis of industrial energy, EPP makes badly flawed assumptions for five key industries, and then generalizes the resulting savings for all other industries. Not only has the project assumed that technology would be available to the degree needed to achieve the forecast savings, but it has also assumed that by 1985 productive capacity and production methods would be rebuilt to the extent necessary to utilize this technology.[p] Furthermore, the savings postulated for these five key industries are dependent not only on rebuilding today's plants but also on creating a new infrastructure (both in terms of facilities and in regulation) for the entire electric industry. According to "Technical Fix" these five industries would cease being purchasers of electricity and become sellers of electricity produced "from their waste heat." Typically, the report goes no further than this claim; *it has not considered whether these dubious electric sales are possible or at what cost to consumers, despite the implication that there would be a requirement to maintain redundant generating capacity.*

Major assumptions have also been made concerning recycling of steel, paper and aluminum, but costs (in both economic and energy terms) of the collection and transportation of this scrap are not included in the simulation, even though recycled aluminum would jump to nearly 50 percent of 1985 consumption in "Zero Energy Growth" as compared with about 25 percent in the "Historical Growth" scenario. Moreover, aluminum consumption in "Technical Fix" is the same as in the "Historical Growth," despite the fact that in the former case some 300 pounds more of aluminum per automobile would be required—equivalent to an understatement of at least 15 percent.

As previously noted, half (or more) of all energy savings in *A Time to Choose* is assigned to the industrial sector. Yet about half of the scenarios' industrial sector savings are accomplished in industries

[p]Many authorities are currently concerned over the ability of the existing economic structure to provide sufficient capital to meet the need for expansion— as well as mandated health, safety, and environmental protection investment requirements. The economics in terms of the capital/fuel trade-offs in each industry were not fully examined by EPP, and the economics of capital availability were not considered at all. For example, the initial cost (made over the years) of plant and equipment of only the steel and paper industries operating at the end of 1974 was $53 billion; the cost of duplicating those facilities, even without modification in design, would be considerably higher in 1974 prices.

other than the five examined in some (limited) detail, so that one-quarter of the total savings (in the entire economy) accrues to *unidentified users* in the industrial section![q]

An important element in these additional savings is assumed reduction in electric process heat (which is treated very much as the report treated assumed saving for electric space heat in residential and commercial sectors). In 1968 this usage was minimal, accounting for only 0.3 Q BTUs. This minor energy use is then assumed to grow fast enough so that by 1985 a total of 2.9 Q BTUs can be saved by reducing it to a more reasonable level. *The saving amounts to half of the energy savings which did not accrue to the five industries noted above* and is greater than the entire energy consumption of the aluminum and cement industries postulated in the "Historical-Growth" case for 1985.

The measures employed in the industrial sector most clearly reveal that "Technical Fix" is not the result of the rational application of existing or new technology, nor is it supported by economics.

Energy Processing

The energy requirements for producing and distributing energy (about 30 percent of all energy) are buried in EPP's discussion of the industrial sector.[r] This is the energy used in generating and delivering electricity, refining oil, shipping natural gas, etc.[s] The only thing that EPP reveals about electricity-generation efficiency is the assumption that it will be improving from the 9900 TBTs required to generate a KWH in 1985 to 9220 in the year 2000. The reader has to find out for himself that these figures also represent significant improvement over the 10,479 BTUs per KWH needed in 1972.[t] The trend in generating efficiency through the late 1960s was one of slow, steady improvement, but thereafter it came to a halt and was reversed by the measures taken to control air pollution.[u] Fuel

----

[q]This 25 percent figure excludes "energy processing industries" which we will discuss separately.

[r]These requirements, 34 Q BTU in the 1985 "Historical Growth" case (about 30 percent of all energy) are allotted only two pages of the 511 pages in *A Time to Choose*.

[s]The energy used up in electricity generation and transmission amounts to 24.5 Q BTU in HG 1985, and the requirements for providing other forms of energy are 9.3 Q BTU.

[t]The historical figures were not analyzed in *A Time to Choose* but are available from the Edison Electric Institute.

[u]The most efficient year was 1968 when 10,371 BTUs were used to generate each KWH.

substitution (to control pollution or in response to import policy) and emission control devices invariably lead to higher energy requirements. Again, EPP refuses to recognize actual trends, once again minimizing "Historical Growth" energy requirements.

A similar situation exists in estimates of the energy required to refine petroleum. Not only would existing refineries have to be rebuilt to be as efficient as the best existing today, but refineries would switch from being purchasers of electricity to being marketers of electricity. The problems of marketing electricity by refineries would be no less than those faced by the five key industries discussed above. It should also be noted that refinery efficiency (as measured by EPP) is not only a function of effective design and operation, but is in large part determined by the kinds of products the refinery produces. In EPP's view, refinery efficiency is measured by the energy used to produce a barrel of output, without regard to what kind of products are required. But to produce different mixes of refinery output requires differing amounts of energy. Refinery product mix is totally disregarded when the most "efficient" refinery is used by EPP as the standard of the future, thus displaying a total lack of concern whether a BTU is in the form of low-sulfur home heating oil, high-sulfur heavy fuel oil, lead-free gasoline or a premium-quality lubricant. The more environmentally desirable products are those which require more intense processing and more energy per unit.

SUMMARY OF *A TIME TO CHOOSE*
ENERGY REDUCTIONS

It is appropriate at this point to summarize the reductions in energy usage involved in reaching the levels in the "Technical Fix" case. For this purpose, table 5–3 begins with the historical trends in energy consumption extended to 1985. These totals (by demand sector) are taken from the table 5–2, at which point the derivation of the trends was discussed.

We have already noted that actual historical trends would require 16.9 Q BTUs more energy in 1985 than the "Historical Growth" scenario pictures.

This number must be kept in mind if one views the adjustments to reduce "Historical Growth" to "Technical Fix" levels. Relatively small amounts of savings are involved in the identified adjustments. In the residential/commercial sector, for example, 1.2 Q BTUs is accounted for by more efficient air-conditioners and furnaces. About a third of the cut in the industrial sector (in the five key industries)

Table 5-3. Energy Usage Reductions to Reach EPP "Technical Fix" (Quadrillion BTU)

| | CONSUMING SECTORS | | | |
	Residential and Commercial	Industrial and Raw Materials	Transportation	Total
Historic Trends Continue	45.2	57.6	30.2	133.0
EPP Shortfall	(7.2)	(5.5)	(4.2)	(16.9)
EPP "Historical Growth"	38.0	52.1	26.0	116.1
Technical Fix Reductions				
Replace Electric Heat	(2.7)	(2.9)		
Improved Insulation and "Belt Tightening"	(2.1)	(2.1)		
More Efficient Air Conditioners and Furnaces	(1.2)			
Automotive Design & Weight			(5.0)	
Slower and More Full Aircraft			(1.2)	
Shift Transportation Modes			(0.2)	
Change Processes in Five Key Industries		(3.9)		
Cogeneration, Steam and Electric		(0.4)		
Reduced Fuel Processing		(2.8)		
SUBTOTAL	(6.0)	(12.1)	(6.4)	(24.5)
Equals "Technical Fix"	32.0	40.0	19.6	91.6[i]
Total Reductions	(13.2)	(17.6)	(10.6)	(41.4)
Percent Reduction from Trends	29.2	30.6	35.1	31.1
Percent Technical Fix Reductions of Total Reductions	45.5	68.8	60.4	59.2

[i]Correct Total; Note, *A Time to Choose*, table 5, was incorrectly added to 91.3. This is noted here to alert the reader to numerous similar discrepancies in *A Time to Choose*.

can be identified. In the case of electrical heat for both residential/ commercial and industrial sectors, *A Time to Choose* assumes that future use of electrical heat would mushroom, making it possible to assume very substantial savings by eliminating much of this growth. As we have previously noted, our view of historical trends does not involve such rapid growth of electric heat in either sector.

The 19.6 Q BTU total for the transportation sector is 35 percent less than the historical trends. It is in this sector that the largest percentage cuts are taken. These cuts arise, not by reason of the application of known technology, but by legislated automobile design, by limiting vehicle usage, and by underestimating the fleet size in 1985 by 6 million or more private passenger cars.[v]

In short, to reach "Technical Fix," the historical trend is reduced about a third by 1985 under the project's assumptions. The greater portion of these assumptions is in reality unspecified.

A Time to Choose devotes much attention to the environmental (especially health) and domestic political demerits of each energy source. It never reaches the point of making the judgment which of these sources is the least undesirable, even though enormous amounts of new energy would be needed in even the lowest-growth scenarios, both for growth and to replace the reserves used up over time. *The impression remains that in EPP's view, the only good energy source is one left undeveloped.*

If *A Time to Choose* had selected even a *tentative* supply structure, questions concerning the relative costs of supply compared with those of conservation could not have been sidestepped. Trade-offs with economic, environmental, national security, and foreign policies would have been tabled by implication. It would then have been impossible to make the environmental chapter of *A Time to Choose* simply a list of negative aspects of each energy form; the requirement for ranking environmental risks could not have been ignored. Thus, *A Time to Choose* avoided displaying any suggestion of specific supply preferences, since that would be a necessary first step towards the reconciliation needed to turn an energy policy debate away from political confrontation and toward analytically sound, constructive compromise. Regardless of which estimates of energy usage might best represent the actual future and regardless of the circumstances that might emerge to determine that usage, it is an exercise in fantasy to discuss energy consumption without serious analysis of supply.

---

[v]*A Time to Choose* estimated that there would be 119 million cars by 1985. NPC projected 140 million cars by 1985, and a recent forecast by one of the project's consultants, DRI, (dated Summer 1976) shows 142.6 million registered cars in 1985; a recently published forecast by DuPont projects a 50 percent increase in the number of automobiles between 1970 and 1985, which would result in a similar total.

Chapter 9 and Big Oil

The tone of chapter 9, which draws a crude caricature of "Big Oil," borders on paranoia. Allegations are plentiful; documentation is nonexistent. Illustrative of this is the treatment of "the exceptional political power" of the industry. There are numerous references to this nebulous power. Page 236 states that the 1959 oil import quota program benefited the industry by causing higher crude oil prices and is immediately followed by: "The influence of the industry in *securing* such programs is investigated later in this chapter." Yet the promised "investigation" (page 243) yields the statement: "Initially the international oil companies opposed import controls."

Similarly, the report admits insufficient data to reach a conclusion that major oil companies squeeze independent producers, but this fact is buried beneath verbiage that clearly leaves the reader with the opposite impression. It concludes: "There seems to be little doubt that the majors' ownership position in the key transportation link of the crude oil business gives them a strategic position in organizing supplies."

The report strongly opposes the energy industry because of the large size of the units within it. "The argument," states a disembodied source (a familiar technique that provides a convenient alter ego where the report strives to appear objective), "is that our institutions that supply energy have grown too large to be responsive to the needs of individuals and society in general." The effect of large institutions in our society is surely an intricate topic, one that encompasses the physical, sociological, and psychological aspects of American life. It is not an effect that we may cavalierly dismiss. It is unclear, however, how a writer who raises the specter of unwieldy, impersonal energy corporations can harbor a predilection toward pervasive intervention by even larger governmental agencies. Yet this is precisely the view of *A Time to Choose*.

As regards the displacement of the private by the public sector in the energy industry, practical experience surely encourages a highly skeptical view. Examples of attempts by other governments at development in the energy industry are available for study by anyone who cares to take the time. There are more than sixty government-controlled companies involved in various facets of the oil industry. Some of them were established for narrow purposes and so can perhaps be excused if they have failed to contribute to the development of energy resources. On the other hand, the only government companies that have been successful in the search for and development of oil and gas resources are those in which the government investment has had a totally passive influence. If we leave aside the two prime examples of companies where government took a passive role in business operation, their record of discoveries of major deposits of hydrocarbons has been dismal. The private oil companies, on the other hand, have continued to press the frontiers of technology and to bring new deposits of oil and gas into production in good times and bad, when prices were high and when prices were low, providing a reliable source of energy to fuel the industrial engines of the developing world.

It should be noted that the competitive pressures upon private industry have resulted in finds of oil which are essential for the long run, even though they might not be important in the short run. The largest U.S. oil field (prior to the discovery of the Prudhoe Bay Field in Alaska), the East Texas Oil Field, was discovered in a time of surplus. This was the result of the free enterprise system at work; individual firms continued to search for oil to improve their competitive position, even though "enough" had already been found. The ability of a government company to spend current tax dollars to search for oil under conditions of surplus must, however, be questioned.

The lack of success on the part of the government oil companies cannot be laid to the ineptitude of a handful of bureaucrats charged with the administration of these companies. We suggest there are several more fundamental reasons. First, the oil industry is a high-risk industry in which the vast majority of the exploratory wells are *not* successful. For any government agency to engage in an effort involving expenditures of public funds where the prospect of success is so slim is a risky political venture, especially since politicians would find most voters would not benefit from the expenditures in the way they do from other government spending programs. Second, the attitudes of governments toward the commitment of funds to an exploration program is different from that of private companies. The private company is necessarily interested in making a profit and, therefore, will commit its funds to the most attractive projects. The government company must also meet public obligations, not the least of which is the need to tailor employment levels to policy considerations for the government, generally, and the need to negotiate appropriations on an annual basis whether or not the business considerations of the project justify the expenditure of money. A third reason has to do with the nature of government agencies, as generally being responsible for the administration of the activity within its own geographical borders. Unfortunately, the search for oil must follow the attractive geological settings and cannot be constrained by national boundaries. Consequently, the government companies are at a disadvantage if they cannot choose to explore beyond their borders, even though the application of information they have learned might well be productive if carried to a different geographic location. Similarly, technology, useful to the search for and extraction of energy resources, cannot yield its full benefit if confined by national boundaries. This obstacle is not easily surmounted; government activity beyond its borders always will involve political as well as economic considerations.

There are other reasons why a government oil company would *not* truly function to meet the other goals which *A Time to Choose* suggests for it—for example, to serve as a "yardstick corporation" or to provide a country with energy independence. If it were to follow the pattern of other government companies, such as the Post Office, the New York subway system, and the Tennessee Valley Authority, a government oil company would have no requirement to earn a profit in order to stay alive. Additionally, it would pay no taxes, no royalties, no rentals, and, in effect, no lease bonuses, since money would be paid out of one "federal pocket" into another. There would be no pressure to obtain an adequate return on capital, thus perhaps forestalling the potential for development of considerable government lands under its control. In fact, a national oil company would not be responsive to many of the conditions that keep private industry efficient. The competitive incentive of each company to develop better geological data, for example, would be absent. Additionally, to the extent that a government company would possess the ability to avoid many of the costs which must be met by private companies, it would gain an extreme competitive advantage. The net result of all this might be an inefficient, subsidized government company which could undercut inherently efficient private oil concerns. Such a "yardstick corporation" would in no sense provide a measure by which to judge the operation of other oil companies; in fact, there is good reason to believe that less, not more, oil reserves would be found and produced.

Chapter 9 of *A Time to Choose* (p. 232) concludes: "The energy supply industries are not overly-concentrated." Though an understatement, it is a true statement. As noted in *A Time to Choose*, the standard rule for judging monopoly power states: if concentration ratios are below 50 percent for the four largest firms in an industry and below 70 percent for the eight largest, the industry is competitive. Concentration ratios in crude oil production, petroleum refining, gasoline sales, natural gas sales and coal production are all well below these yardstick measures. Concentration ratios for total energy production in 1970 were a mere 21 percent for the top four firms and 35 percent for the top eight. For crude oil production, these figures are 31 percent and 50 percent.

After noting these facts, Chapter 9 continues with generalizations that seemingly cast doubt on the viability of the statistics. For example, they state: "Concentration ratios have been increasing sharply in some branches of the industry—particularly in crude oil and coal production." They neglect to point out that in petroleum refining and marketing, concentration ratios have actually decreased. The reader is left with the impression that concentration ratios are indeed steeply higher. The project, notes that, in the 1955-70 period, ". . . petroleum companies acquired $337 million of the assets of independent petroleum marketers and refiners." It should have noted, however, that one of their own consultants had put total assets (U.S.) for the petroleum industry in 1971 at $84 billion. Thus, the multimillion dollar figure noted above, when put in perspective, amounts to less than one-half of 1 percent of total domestic industry assets. Additionally, no mention is made of the fact that divestment of assets by major oil companies far exceeded acquisition of small company assets in the 1955-70 period.

Indeed, the remainder of Chapter 9 is full of misleading verbiage. After a cursory examination of the trend on the part of some oil companies to invest in other energy sources and after about two paragraphs of specious statements regarding reserve ownership, page 234 states: "If one company dominated supplies of all three sources of fuel, there would be no competitive safeguard and that company could set the prices it wished." The statement reads as though such an event is inevitable, ignoring the fact that no one company dominates *any* fuel. *In fact, the largest eight companies do not control the supply of either coal, gas or oil.*[a]

A Time to Choose concludes at one point that entry into energy industries is moderately free, but the report is replete with other statements implying there is no freedom of entry. In fact, the independent companies have done well and have increased their position over time. There are more U.S. refining companies today with capacity in excess of 50,000 barrels per day than there were in 1951, and eleven of them were not even in the refining business in 1951. On the marketing side, publicly available data show that independents moved from 22.5 percent of the U.S. market in 1967 to 30.6 percent in the first quarter of 1974. Also lost in the verbiage describing Exxon Corporation's purchase of coal is the fact that the nation's largest coal company was bought by a metal company, not an oil company, and the nation's largest concentration of coal reserves is not in private hands, but in the hands of the government.

On the international scene, the growth of newcomers has also been spectacular. In exploration and production, refining, marketing, and transportation sectors, there is a sharp contrast between activity in 1953 and that which existed in 1972. In 1953, thirty-three American companies possessed foreign exploration rights, and by 1972, 330 separate companies held exploration rights to over 6.8 million square miles of land. In 1953, no company, other than the seven largest, had foreign oil production greater than 200,000 daily barrels, while fourteen new companies had passed this level by 1972. Similarly, entrance of newcomers into the refining sector of the foreign oil industry has been rapid, with 55 percent of the new refining capacity constructed in the period 1953–72 having been built by new companies. In marketing, more than twenty companies other than the seven largest made substantial progress toward becoming international petroleum marketers by 1972. Similarly, in transportation, the major oil companies owned only 28 percent of the world's tanker fleet in 1953, and their share had declined to 19 percent by 1972. Chase Manhattan Bank data show that during the period 1953 to 1972 the annual foreign capital expenditures of new companies rose faster than those of the five largest U.S. oil companies. In his book *Multi-National Oil*, Neil Jacoby estimates that 350 "new internationals" entered the oil industry in the 1953 to 1972 period. As he states: "This clearly refutes the idea that an effective cartel of seven companies was in operation during this period."

[a]*A Time to Choose*, p. 231.

If EPP's treatment of competitiveness of the oil industry in economic terms is faulty, its "analysis" of the industry's political power is surely a gross oversimplification of the complex relationship between a multi-faceted industry and countless governmental regulatory and administrative bodies, as well as a gross exaggeration of this so-called political power. Chapter 9 promises much but delivers little in the form of documentation of alleged industry control of government. For example, page 242 states: "A mass of favorable legislative and administrative programs attest to the effectiveness of the oil industry's long history of involvement in the political process."

Similarly, page 236 claims: "The industry benefited from government price support programs." However, the "mass" of administrative programs apparently consists primarily of the oil import program; there is no discussion of price controls at all. In fact, as A Time to Choose observes, the international oil companies actually opposed that type of import controls, and the operation of the quota system favored the independent refiners over the majors by awarding them a more than proportionate share of cheap imported supplies.

Similarly, treatment of the tax system as it applies to energy corporations is greatly oversimplified and delivered in an argumentative style as though, if all were as it should be, such tax programs should not exist. The report is particularly weak in its discussion of the foreign tax credit, a subject which involves questions of international competition and equity in international taxation affecting all industries (not solely those industries dealing with resource extraction) and which carries broad implications for balance of payments and foreign policy. Indeed, the study's very definition of the foreign tax credit is misstated. On page 247, it is stated: "The U.S. tax law allows a credit against corresponding U.S. income tax liability for foreign income taxes already paid." This is untrue. United States tax law clearly prohibits any offset by foreign taxes of taxes on income earned in the U.S.

Page 249 continues: "A survey of legislative and administrative regulations discloses that in only one case have the oil companies not been effective in imposing their wishes in the field of industry regulation—that of natural gas prices." This "survey" somehow neglected the fact that oil is the only industry whose prices are still controlled long after the last price controls (which were imposed in all industries in 1971) have been removed on every other product in the economy; with the passage of the 1975 Energy Act, we are assured of at least another forty months of controls. Ignored is the fact that the oil industry is regulated more than any other non-utility industry. Innumerable governmental administrative agencies, congressional committees, and executive departments oversee the daily functioning of the oil industry and monitor movements of energy and energy prices. In fact, one of the project's own publications, *Energy Research & Development*, enumerated the profusion of government agencies which have extensive power over the industry. And what of the regulation of natural gas prices? How has this served the nation? The resultant underpricing of gas has distorted end uses (thereby misallocating this clean fuel, on an economic and environmental basis) and stunted supplies (with the resultant shortages now apparent).

Continual reference is made to the absolute size of the oil industry and certain companies in particular. For example, on page 230 it is stated: "Oil companies' incomes eclipse the wealth of states and nations." However, it simply does not follow that the size of a company or industry implies enormous political power to further economic goals. Indeed, the Alaskan pipeline project is a paramount example of the inequality inherent in the EPP's economic-political equation. If there was any individual project for which allegedly "all-powerful" political influence should have been evident if it existed, it would have been this project. The facts, however, are that the pipeline has been delayed by years beyond any reasonable construction period. This is surely not the mark of the exercise of great power. Indeed, some individuals who became involved in the Energy Policy Project had the greater power; they did succeed in delaying the project and enormously increasing its costs.

In its treatment of the relationship of antitrust to oil corporations, *A Time to Choose* states: "We find no basis at present to suggest the breakup of the majors into constituent parts." There then follows a discussion of the lack of success enjoyed by the Justice Department in prosecuting the industry, concluding with the following statement: "What concerns us is that they (the resolution of the Justice Department actions) all led to the same result—a failure to rigidly enforce the anti-trust laws." It is hard to understand what *A Time to Choose* would have the government do: on one hand it states that the industry is clearly competitive; but on the other, it agonizes over what it perceives to be a lack of enforcement of the antitrust laws. There is no doubt that oil companies today are confronted by a lack of credibility,[b] but simply repeating allegations and

[b]There are several understandable reasons for these circumstances. The size of the job to be done requires large corporations (even though the share of the industry held by the largest is smaller than in many other industries), and bigness

suspicions can only heighten tensions in our society, while offering no constructive resolution of energy problems.

creates fear. The business of finding, developing, refining, marketing, and moving petroleum involves complicated interrelationships between functions and complex technology. It is not easily understood by nonexperts and people tend to be suspicious of that which they do not understand. The petroleum industry is subject to a tremendous number of laws, rules, and regulations by a great many levels of government and their agencies. The principal product bought by the public, gasoline, is among the most highly taxed. Thus, the appearance that the industry presents to the public is in large part determined by government, an anomaly both hard to explain and understand when the consumer is unhappy with the price of a product he seemingly purchases from a "private enterprise" firm.

Appendix A

Some Specific Failures of the EPP's Economic Analysis

The EPP retained Data Resources Inc. (DRI) to provide the economic analyses required to support the contention that there need be but little linkage between the rate of energy consumption and the health of the economy. Both EPP and the consultant (DRI) freely acknowledged the constraints placed upon the analysis. The consultant had to fit its model to the "Historical Growth" scenario. The consultants had to take the major EPP assumptions as "given" and were limited to macroeconomic analysis of unusually aggregated data while being steered away from any meaningful microeconomic interpretation. This appendix examines some of the specifics of the assumptions and "calibrations" that lead to EPP's superficial claim that economics show "TF" and "ZEG" "conservation" to be easy and nearly costless.

The first and most obvious contrivance is the use of a new kind of Gross National Product, one which superficially seems to grow at a healthy (but not vigorous) pace (table A-1, line 1). But this Gross National Product is not the concept usually used in economic discussions; to normal Gross National Product there has been added a new item, "services of durables" (A-1, line 2). This novel addition to the National Income Accounts includes the imputed flow of services to consumers from "the automobile and other home and personal appliances" which he already owns. Should we really believe that somehow the stock of consumer durable goods, made and distributed in earlier years, provides employment this year? Or is it that the Energy Policy Project feels the real value of the services delivered by the possessions we already have will increase rapidly

Table A-1. *A Time to Choose:* **Scenarios for the Economy**

	1975	1985	2000	Growth Rates (%/Yr.) 1975-1985	1985-2000	MEMO 1960-1973
1. *EPP Gross Product* (EPP Concept) (Billion 1971$)						
Historical Growth	1442.2	2049.2[iii]	3342.0[iii]	3.6	3.3	N.A.
Technical Fix	1442.2	2019.0[iii]	3218.5	3.4	3.2	N.A.
Zero Energy Growth	1442.2	1029.9[iii]	3226.7	3.4	3.2	N.A.
2. *Services of Durables* (EPP Concept) (Billion 1971$)						
HG, TF, ZEG	142.6	226.6	446.8	4.7	4.6	N.A.
3. *EPP Gross National Product* (Standard Concept) (Billion 1971$)[i]						
Historical Growth	1299.6	1822.6	2895.2	3.4	3.1	4.3
Technical Fix	1299.6	1792.4	2771.7	3.3	2.9	4.3
Zero Energy Growth	1299.6	1793.3	2779.9	3.3	3.0	4.3
4. *EPP Personal Consumption* (EPP Concept) (Billion 1971$)						
Historical Growth	838.3	1211.8	1990.9	3.8	3.4	N.A.
Technical Fix	838.3	1188.2	1904.5	3.6	3.2	N.A.
Zero Energy Growth	838.3	1185.3	1885.4	3.5	3.2	N.A.
5. *EPP Personal Consumption* (Standard Concept) (Billion 1971$)[ii]						
Historical Growth	695.7	985.2	1544.1	3.5	3.0	4.4
Technical Fix	695.7	961.6	1457.7	3.3	2.8	4.4
Zero Energy Growth	695.7	958.7	1438.6	3.3	2.7	4.4
6. *EPP Employment* (Billion Man-hours)						
Historical Growth	170.546[iii]	205.103	262.557	1.9	1.7	1.6
Technical Fix	170.546[iii]	205.324[iii]	262.436[iii]	1.9	1.7	1.6
Zero Energy Growth	170.546[iii]	205.792[iii]	274.334[iii]	1.9	1.9	1.6
7. *Output per Man-hour* (Billion 1971 $)[iv]						
Historical Growth	7.62	8.88	11.03	1.5	1.5	2.7
Technical Fix	7.62	8.72	10.56	1.4	1.3	2.7
Zero Energy Growth	7.62	8.71	10.13	1.3	1.0	2.7
8. *Consumption per Man-hour* (Billion 1971$)[v]						
Historical Growth	4.08	4.80	5.88	1.6	1.4	2.8
Technical Fix	4.08	4.68	5.55	1.4	1.1	2.8
Zero Energy Growth	4.08	4.66	5.24	1.4	0.8	2.8
9. *EPP Employment* (Million Persons)						
HG, TF, ZEG	87.2	103.0	121.2	1.7	1.1	1.9
10. *EPP Average Work Week* (hours)[vi]						
Historical Growth	37.6	38.3	41.6	0.2	0.6	(0.3)
Technical Fix	37.6	38.3	41.6	0.2	0.6	(0.3)
Zero Energy Growth	37.6	38.4	43.5	0.2	0.8	(0.3)

i   = line 1 less line 2
ii = line 4 less line 2
iii = Differs from Appendix F Tables F-2, F-3, F-6 due to use of conventional addition rules.
iv = line 3 ÷ line 6
v   = line 5 ÷ line 6
vi = line 6 ÷ (line 9 × 52)
N.A. = Published data are not available on this basis.

because there will be a scarcity of replacement items? Whatever the case, the "services of durables" must be removed in order for the reader to see more clearly in a normal frame of reference the happy economic future that the project plans. Alas, the future is not so happy, even in their "Historical Energy Growth" case (table A-1, line 3).

In our published dissent to the Preliminary Report of the Energy Policy Project, we objected to the "Historical Energy Growth" figures because they were not truly a continuation of the trends of the recent past. We now find the support for our objection in the Data Resources, Inc. analysis, which in its appendix F to *A Time to Choose*, as we noted previously, had to "calibrate" the model in order to produce the historical growth path and thus had to start with a relatively low growth for Gross National Product. The project's alleged economic growth for the 1975-85 period is 3.6 percent a year, but converting it to the more normal concept of GNP, the growth is less than 3.4 percent per year. The words *relatively low* are used here both in the historical context (real Gross National Product grew 4.3 percent per year from 1960 to 1973) and in the context of the standard forecast that Data Resources, Inc. was providing at about the same time to general subscribers to its long-term forecasting service (that forecast was 4.1 percent per year for 1975-85). Clearly, the assumptions and parameters that the Energy Policy Project required Data Resources, Inc. to use in starting their analysis were already restraining the economic growth model. Even masking this with a rapidly growing "services of durables" could not produce a very strong long-term economic picture.

The "Historical Growth" concept of personal consumption (table A-1, line 4), similarly is not the conventional measure. Subtracting out the services of previously acquired durable goods (table A-1, line 2) reduces the growth rate for the next ten years from 3.8 percent to 3.5 percent per year (line 5). This is a much less satisfactory outlook than would be expected from the experience of the recent past, when between 1960 and 1973 personal consumption rose 4.4 percent per year.

These differences in growth rate may, at first glance, appear minor, but it is necessary to look at these facts first if we care to judge the claims in chapter 6 of full and productive employment. Appendix F provides estimates of how many hours people of this country will have to work (A-1, line 6) to achieve these less than optimum results. We all can, of course, accept the fact that the favorable standard of living in this country and its growth are a direct result of high and growing productivity from our labors. Some measure of the productivity gains *A Time to Choose* implies for the future can be derived from the Data Resources, Inc. appendix by dividing real GNP by the man-hours required to produce it (table A-1, line 7). This shows that even in the most favorable case, productivity is substantially retarded. In the "Historical Growth" case, it would grow 1.5 percent per year and in the other cases as low as 1.0 percent per year—dramatically less than the 2.7 percent per year the American people became accustomed to in the 1960 to 1973 period. This is of immense importance to the social well-being of this country, because the real motor driving increasing standard of living for the least economically advantaged groups in this country has been economic growth (despite all the income redistribution policies introduced in the past fifteen years). The essence of economic growth is rising productivity: without it, gains could be but little more than rate of population increase.

How would *A Time to Choose* compensate the employees of this economy for their labors? We are not provided with compensation figures, but over the long term consumption parallels income, and thus a glimpse of the *A Time to Choose* future can be obtained by dividing personal consumption by the man-hours required to earn it (table A-1, line 8). In the best future we are offered, consumption per man-hour increases 1.6 percent per year; in the worst case it falls to a stunted 0.8 percent per year. This is in sharp contrast to expectations based on the 2.8 percent per year growth realized in the 1960–73 era.

Since *A Time to Choose* promises a job for almost anyone who wants one (labor force participation rates grow rapidly), perhaps there is some solace to be found in more leisure in the future and the reason for the stunted economy is that we will not work as hard and as long. Alas, this illusion is quickly shattered by a peek beneath the surface of the study's economic future. Dividing the man-hour figure presented in Appendix F (table A-1, line 6) by the number of people shown as employed in Chapter 6 (table A-1, line 9) reveals that the average work week (table A-1, line 10) suddenly ends its very long-term historical decline in 1975 and then increases rapidly. In the year 2000, the average worker in the "Historical Growth" case would be putting in four more hours a week than in 1975. In the "Zero Energy Growth" case, he would have to put in an extra six hours. Simply put, if energy usage is excessively curtailed, growth in productivity is cut. To reach a given output, people would have to work longer. This, then, is the real nature of the concept of the future in *A Time to Choose*.

What do these "moderate" and "non-trivial" differences in growth rates (Table A-2) really mean? First, the difference between the 4.1 percent per year Gross National Product forecast for 1975–85

Table A-2. Comparison of Cost to the Economy of EPP Scenarios

			Cumulative	
			1975–	*1985–*
EPP Gross National Product (Billion 1971$)	*1985*	*2000*	*1985*	*2000*
Historical Growth vs. Technical Fix	-30.2	-123.5	-151.0	-1152.8
Historical Growth vs. Zero Energy Growth	-29.3	-115.3	-146.5	-1084.5
Technical Fix vs. Zero Energy Growth	+0.9	+8.2	+4.5	+68.2
EPP Personal Consumption (Billion 1971$)				
Historical Growth vs. Technical Fix	-23.6	-86.4	-118.0	-825.0
Historical Growth vs. Zero Energy Growth	-26.5	-105.5	-132.5	-990.0
Technical Fix vs. Zero Energy Growth	-2.9	-19.1	-14.5	-165.0

(given by Data Resources, Inc. to general subscribers) and the "Historical Growth" projection of 3.4 percent per year means that the 1985 economy would be $182 billion smaller in the "Historical Growth" case, a cumulative loss during the ten years of $900 billion. But since the frame of reference in *A Time to Choose* starts with the "Historical Growth" as the base case, let us compute the costs (output loss) of going from "Historical Growth" to "Technical Fix" or "Zero Energy Growth". The *additional* cost to the economy of cutting energy supply from "Historical Growth" to "Technical Fix" is $30 billion in the year 1985 and $123 billion in the year 2000, resulting in a cumulative loss of $150 billion by 1985 and a cumulative loss of $1.3 trillion by the year 2000 (1975–2000). To place this last figure in context, table 12 of *A Time to Choose* tells us that the U.S. economy would benefit by saving a net $285 billion in the last twenty-five years of this century through the lower capital requirements for energy (net of capital for conservation) in the "Technical Fix" case vs. the "Historical Growth" case. Thus, if we net that figure from the cumulative loss in Gross National Product between the cases, we would still have $1 trillion left in costs. Truly, the Energy Policy Project has missed the chance to tell us of an enormous opportunity for applying capital to reduce the environmental impact of energy consumption. The policies that would lead the economy to an "Historical Growth" or an even better economic future could also see much of the added output applied to reducing environmental disturbance.

What kinds of jobs will be available in the economy of *A Time to Choose?* Here we are given practically no answer, and what we are given is, at best, mysterious. The largest, and by far the fastest growing, sector of employment is "services and government," but nowhere is it explained what this includes.[a] But whatever the case, about two-thirds of employment in *A Time to Choose* economy is in the "services and government" category, and that is the growth sector for the future. Unfortunately, a categorization so gross and undifferentiated is not a useful basis for analysis. It includes employment in industries that are energy-intensive and employment in others that are not. It includes the kinds of employment with no productivity growth. To put it mildly, it is astounding to find, in an analysis of economic growth, workers in construction, mining, and utilities in the same sector as those employed by government or even in the same sector as lawyers, doctors, and barbers.

Thus, after exposing the nature of what *A Time to Choose* seems to mean by services (and this includes government), we are left with the strong suspicion that most of future growth in employment will be by government. This suspicion is confirmed in two other ways. First, the very low growth in productivity, revealed in preceding paragraphs, must be because there is projected a greater share of employment in the no-productivity-growth areas. There has not been and cannot be real growth in government worker productivity in the macro-economic sense, by commonly accepted definition. Second, the stunted nature of economic growth in these low-energy consumption models would have to be as a result of a shift away from the productive activities that are more dependent on energy.

Not more than a superficial understanding of the interdependent nature of the U.S. economy is required to know that the 10.3 percent figure for energy intensive employment is a misrepresentation.[b] In table A-4, we have identified only those industries where employment is most obviously impacted if growth of the economy is retarded by inadequate energy. (It does not include employment in the hotel and recreation industries, business service industries or general merchandise retailing, all of which would be impacted by energy conditions that stunt potential economic growth.) As we have previously shown, the real message of the Data Resources, Inc. analysis is that inadequate energy can stunt the economy. The areas of high productivity growth will be affected most in such

---

[a]We have attempted to find historical data that would align with the projections given in *A Time to Choose* for each of their five subdivisions of employment (see Table A-3). The data contained in our table do not precisely align with their definitions, and we cannot be sure whether it is a problem of the grossness of the categories used by the Energy Policy Project or whether it is more a matter of their lack of care for detail (which allowed their tables to remain incorrectly tallied).

[b]*A Time to Choose*, table 32, p. 144.

Table A-3   Shares of Employment (Percent)

	1929[i]	1948[i]	1969[i]	H.G. 1975[ii]	TECH 1975[iii]	ZEG 1975[iv]	H.G. 1985[ii]	TECH 1985[iii]	ZEG 1985[iv]	H.G. 2000[ii]	TECH 2000[iii]	ZEG 2000[iv]
Contract Construction	5.0	5.5	5.4									
Mining	2.2	1.8	0.8									
Electric, Gas, Sanitary Utilities	1.1	0.9	0.9									
Telephone and Broadcasting	1.2	1.3	1.3									
Bank, Finance, Insurance, Etc.	3.4	3.3	4.5									
Wholesale Trade	3.8	4.5	4.7									
Retail Trade	}13.1	13.8	13.9									
Automotive Services		0.6	0.6									
Misc. Repair Services	0.3	0.4	0.4									
Hotels, etc.	1.1	1.1	1.0									
Motion Pictures and Amusements	1.0	0.9	0.9									
Personal Services	2.2	2.1	1.8									
Misc. Business Services	}}0.6	0.7	2.0									
Misc. Professional Services		0.5	1.0									
Medical & Health[v]	1.1	1.1	1.9									
Educational Services[v]	0.2	0.2	0.2									
Legal (v)	0.4	0.4	0.5									
Private Households	5.1	2.7	1.7									
Non Profit Organizations	1.9	2.7	5.3									
Government & Government Enterprises	6.7	12.3	17.9									
Total Services & Government[vi]	50.4	56.8	66.7	61.9	61.9	61.9	63.3	63.4	63.5	64.0	54.2	65.5
Agriculture	19.9	11.0	4.3	9.7	9.7	9.7	9.6	9.6	9.6	9.9	9.9	9.5
Manufacturing	23.1	27.1	25.7	24.4	24.4	24.4	23.4	23.3	23.3	22.8	22.7	21.9
Transportation	6.6	5.1	3.3	4.0	4.0	4.0	3.7	3.7	3.6	3.3	3.2	3.1
Total Economy	100.0	100.0	100.0	100.0	100.0	100.0	100.0	100.0	100.0	100.0	100.0	100.0

i   Survey of Current Business, Oct., 1973
ii A Time To Choose, p. 498
iii Ibid., p. 502
iv Ibid., p. 508
v   Provided by "Business Sector" (i.e., non-government)
vi As Defined by the Energy Policy Project.

Table A-4. Recent Shares of U.S. Employment (Percent) Industries with a High Relationship to Energy Availability

Manufacturing -	Durable Goods	15.1
	Paper and Printing	2.3
	Chemicals	1.4
	Oil and Coal Products	0.2
	Rubber and Plastic Products	0.8
Wholesale -	Motor Vehicles	0.4
	Drugs, Chemicals	0.3
	Electrical Goods	0.4
	Hardware	0.2
	Machinery, Equipment	0.9
Retail -	Building Materials	0.7
	Auto Dealers, Gas Stations	2.0
	Furniture, etc.	0.6
Contract Construction		5.4
Mining		0.8
Electric, Gas, Utilities		0.9
Transportation		3.3
	Total	35.7

circumstances. Thus, the number of jobs exposed to energy uncertainty is obviously 300 to 400 percent more than the figure claimed by *A Time to Choose*, and this is just the tip of the iceberg.

❋ *Part II*

A Time to Choose: A Reply

Carl Kaysen

Section 1

The Basic Validity of
A Time to Choose

Mr. Tavoulareas and his colleagues at Mobil have given us a mixed bag of polemical rhetoric, political commentary, and specific criticisms of the projections and calculations of *A Time to Choose*. Rather than trying to deal individually with each point Mr. Tavoulareas makes, we will discuss what we take to be the three principal themes in his critique: (1) *A Time to Choose* does a disservice by not recognizing that accelerating the increase of energy supply is not only possible but is clearly preferable to constraining the growth of demand; (2) *A Time to Choose* takes an antibusiness, antimarket, antigrowth ideological stance, which it defends with too much loaded rhetoric and too little careful analysis; and, most important of all, (3) the quantitative analysis underlying the scenarios used in *A Time to Choose* is seriously flawed.

If these criticisms were all correct, or if Mr. Tavoulareas were the only participant in the Energy Policy Project to comment on the several imperfections of the EPP, the tone of outrage that characterizes his critique might have some justification. But, as we show below, most of his criticisms are unfounded; and those with some basis have been made already by the advisory board and published in *A Time to Choose*. We find no evidence here that Mr. Tavoulareas was correct in arguing that the comments of an oil company representative deserved more space than those of the other members of

[a]This reply was prepared by Carl Kaysen with the assistance of Robert H. Williams, who was responsible for much of the analysis underlying the original projections in *A Time to Choose*.

the advisory board; moreover, we conclude that Mr. Tavoulareas and his colleagues have not countered the principal conclusions of the EPP and have revealed no new philosophical, analytical, or policy criticism of the final report.

INCREASING SUPPLY VS.
REDUCING DEMAND

Mr. Tavoulareas presents us with what he calls "the" alternative to the energy conserving strategy presented by *A Time to Choose*. He asserts that our resources and technology permit us to increase energy supply sufficiently to return to a situation of energy surplus, thus holding prices down and preserving both freedom of consumer choice and the proper relation between governmental and business institutions.

Mr. Tavoulareas' supply-oriented policy alternative is clearly preferable only if one accepts the hidden premise that all obstacles to this choice arise from inappropriate and counterproductive government activity: unnecessary controls, inappropriate environmental standards, and other hindrances to a sustained and effortful action by the business sector to develop new energy resources and technologies. But this is hardly the case. Mr. Tavoulareas's assertions ignore three fundamentally inescapable sets of fact. First, there are real resource limitations, especially with respect to readily accessible and conveniently usable sources of energy; as Mobil's ads so persuasively argue, it is getting harder to find and produce the stuff. Second, there are important and growing environmental costs involved in increasing energy use. And third, there are real economic and political costs involved in being dependent on foreign energy supplies.

An unregulated market of the sort sought by Mr. Tavoulareas might, in theory, handle the resource limitation problem, by pricing all energy at the cost of producing the incremental unit of energy—a solution that would probably drastically reduce the rate of growth of energy consumption, would certainly generate sizable "windfall" profits for the energy industry, and, even with special taxes to capture these profits, has yet to be accepted politically. But even in theory, the unaided market cannot price energy to cover environmental costs or the social costs of foreign dependence. When these costs are ignored and market prices are too low, energy consumption and its related environmental damage and import dependence are too high; then, extramarket mechanisms—i.e., government interventions in the market—are required to help find the right balance between supply and demand. This obviously does not mean that every governmental environmental requirement or allocation formula will always be perfectly justified or optimally applied. But it does mean that there are important issues, not merely questionable motives and defective judgment, which explain why some people reach conclusions different from Mr. Tavoulareas on the relative merits of supply expansion and demand reduction.

It is true, as Mr. Tavoulareas points out, that even effective conservation strategies will still leave us with the need to develop new energy sources, and that *A Time to Choose* has disappointingly little to say on which of the supply options we should develop and how; this defect is pointed out quite strongly in the published comments of the advisory board and several of its individual members. But this does not weaken the principal conclusion of *A Time to Choose*— that energy conservation should be a central element of any sensible energy policy, if only so that we have time to consider more carefully the supply decisions we will eventually make.

THE IDEOLOGICAL STANCE OF
A TIME TO CHOOSE

This critique attacks what its author sees as the ideological stance of *A Time to Choose:* on the one hand, hostility toward business and the market, and devaluation if not outright denial of the virtues of free consumer choice and the beneficence of high rates of growth in output and consumption; on the other hand, blind belief in the efficacy of government regulation and control, puritanical joy in abstinence, and delight in conservation as an end in itself.

A Time to Choose itself contains enough explosive rhetoric to have helped set off this counterblast, particularly in chapter 9, dealing with the energy industry. Mr. Tavoulareas's criticism of that chapter is justified in substance, if bombastic in tone. But it is also old stuff; it was all said before in the written comments of members of the advisory board, which were published as a part of the EPP report. (See especially the comments by Minor S. Jameson, Joseph Rensch, Harvy Brooks and Carl Kaysen, and of course, Mr. Tavoulareas himself.) These statements, and many of the subsequent reviewers of the EPP report, have roundly criticized the report for these excesses: as the Brooks-Kaysen comment said; "The populist speech writer seems at times to have taken over from the analyst."

Perhaps the EPP report really does deserve yet another good thumping on this flaw; if so, it will have to wait for a critique that is not itself as ideological as the material it seeks to counter.

Mr. Tavoulareas's faith in the market and aversion to governmental interference have few apparent limits. But the unaided and unimpeded workings of the market simply cannot serve adequately to assure an adequate supply of energy *and* balance national and international security considerations against those of cost. Nor can it balance the possibilities of conservation—including some that would involve substantial changes in the habits and attitudes of the using public and could not be counted on reliably to result from market forces alone—with the opportunities for, and costs of, enlarging supply. And finally, to repeat, it does not and cannot balance the social costs of environmental degradation with the individual benefits of more and cheaper energy, or the social benefits of higher rates of economic growth.

These are inevitably matters that involve collective choice, conflicting views and claims over the range of possible choice and the most desirable outcomes. Decisions of this character and complexity cannot be resolved by the market mechanism in any proper sense. To be sure, they could be left to the discretion of some actors in the situation, e.g., energy producers. Usually, however, in our society they are resolved through the political process. As Mr. Tavoulareas, himself, notes, "Our private enterprise system . . . has come a long way from the days of laissez faire capitalism." Nor is political intervention a novelty in energy markets; quite the contrary, it has been characteristic of their history at least since the First World War. In view of the importance of energy to the society, and the complexity and multinational character of energy supply and demand, the important questions that need discussion are what kind of intervention, how much, and to what purpose. Unfortunately, Mr. Tavoulareas's critique brings nothing specific, novel, or useful either to this discussion, or to the criticism of *A Time to Choose.*

The discussion in section 3 makes much of the lack of decision on problems of energy policy in the several years since the end of the EPP. As we have already said, the unaided market cannot make these decisions appropriately. That the political processes have not made these reflects, among other factors, the complexities of the problem in general, the conflicting values and interests involved, and, more specifically, the unwillingness of political decision-makers to settle for the particular policies that Mr. Tavoulareas recommends.

THE EPP SCENARIOS

Finally, we come to the most detailed of Mr. Tavoulareas's criticisms, those attacking the accuracy, consistency, and realism of the scenarios on which EPP based its analysis. Section 5 of the critique makes five specific charges concerning the energy demand projections in *A Time to Choose:*

1. That the Historical Growth Energy Projections are not "true" historical growth projections; that the 116 Quads* level of demand shown for 1985 already contains reductions from the "true" historical trends and that therefore, the further savings in the Technical Fix and Zero Energy Growth scenario involve double counting.
2. That the Historical Growth scenario underestimates future energy demand because it ignores the force of underlying trends in housing, commercial area expansion, the number and use of cars, environmental protection demands, and the shift to greater electrification.
3. That much of the potential energy saving shown in *A Time to Choose* is unjustified because EPP made a gross overestimate of future electricity consumption for heating purposes and achieved large and easy savings by merely substituting heat pumps or direct use of fuels for resistance heat in these projections.
4. That many of the conservation measures indicated as being technically and economically feasible are unrealistic.
5. That the proposed implementation schedules for significant conservation measures in industry are unrealistic.

The quantitative consequences of these alleged errors are summarized in table 5-3. In section 2 below we address each of these allegations in detail, and show that they are simply wrong, or else reflect assumptions and judgments about matters on which EPP is clearly in better company than is Mobil.

Mr. Tavoulareas is clearly wrong when he asserts that the EPP Historical Growth projection demonstrably underestimates what "true" historical growth is and that therefore there is a substantial unexplained residue of increased demand which must be eliminated to achieve the levels of energy usage shown by the alternate scenarios of *A Time to Choose.* Despite the misleading table 5-1, EPP was not alone in daring to project an Historical Growth energy demand below 120 Quads in 1985. Several major projections, made earlier or about the same time and comparable to the EPP Historical Growth case in their assumptions about world oil prices, produced figures that were about the same as EPP's:

*One Quad equals one quadrillion Btu.

	1985 Projection
EPP, Historical Growth Scenario, 1974	116 Quads
Brookhaven National Lab, 1972	117 Quads
(Reference Energy System)	
U.S. Department of Interior, 1972	117 Quads
FEA, *Project Independence Report*, 1974	118 Quads
(Imports @ $4/barrel)	

Further, as we explain in section 2 a recent and highly detailed study shows even lower projections of energy use for 1985.

Criticisms (2) and (3) amount to little more than the assertion that the assumptions and projections used by the National Petroleum Council are better than the ones used by EPP. The EPP analysts had access to the NPC report, to the sources from which the NPC drew much of its data, to other sources in the literature, and to some original data collection and analysis that EPP itself commissioned, and we see no a priori reason to accept Mr. Tavoulareas's preference for NPC assumptions. On review, the EPP assumptions appear at least as plausible as those of NPC.

Specific examples indicate that EPP used careful judgment in choosing among data sources: for automobiles on the road in 1985, EPP used a Federal Highway Administration estimate (corrected for a smaller population) of 119 million, while NPC assumed 140 million; for projections of electrical heating, EPP used electric industry projections rather than petroleum industry projections; for estimates of the energy costs of pollution control, EPP commissioned a study that concluded they would be small, while NPC assumed they would be large. It may be natural for Mr. Tavoulareas and his colleagues in the petroleum industry to rely heavily on the National Petroleum Council, but that does not make everybody wrong who goes elsewhere for data.

Similar comments apply to criticisms (4) and (5), concerning the technical and economic feasibility of some conservation measures, and the speed with which they can realistically be put into effect. Mr. Tavoulareas is bearish, Mr. Freeman is bullish on conservation opportunities. All we can say is that Mr. Freeman is not alone, and that *A Time to Choose* (along with several of the back-up volumes) persuades us that Mr. Tavoulareas may be in for some big surprises. Further, if one looks past the technical details and asks only whether there are analyses other than EPP that support the idea that energy conservation can be important soon, the answer is clearly yes. For example, the "conservation scenarios" projected by FEA and ERDA, which (with high oil prices) are comparable in spirit to the EPP Technical Fix scenario, yield very similar projections for 1985:

EPP, Technical Fix Scenario, 1974	92 Quads
FEA, *Project Independence Report*, 1974 (Imports @ $11/barrel)	94 Quads
FEA, *National Energy Outlook*, 1976 (Imports @ $13/barrel)	93 Quads
ERDA-48, *Creating Energy Choices*, 1975	97 Quads

Mr. Tavoulareas and his colleagues may still be right, of course, but it is no longer just *A Time to Choose* with which they must contend.

CONCLUSIONS

It is clear to us that *A Time to Choose* was a timely and useful book, which performed a real service by helping to make energy conservation a respectable subject for analysis and policy. The book does have some of the faults Mr. Tavoulareas says it has: it is unhelpful for choosing among supply options; too willing to replace the market with the administrator; one-sided in both its praise for conservation and its attacks on the oil industry. But its technical analyses and its principal message stand up well under careful scrutiny and, indeed, look better and better as history and comparable analyses accumulate.

Further Responses to the Critique

The critique by Mr. Tavoulareas and his colleagues challenges various elements of the energy demand calculations in *A Time to Choose*. In the following pages we examine these criticisms and provide detailed responses to enable the reader to judge the legitimacy of the charges.

IS THE HISTORICAL GROWTH SCENARIO REALLY INCONSISTENT WITH OTHER ANALYTICALLY SOUND PROJECTIONS?

In putting together the list of "available projections of energy requirements" (table 5-1), the authors of the critique give the misleading impression that the EPP projection of 116 Quads for 1985 is not only the lowest of the range of available estimates, but that the difference between it and the other projections ranges from 4 to 36 Quads. Little is said about the quality of these other estimates (except the NPC projections), and worse, the Mobil authors leave off their list several of the most significant and detailed projections. The following are other important studies conducted prior to the publication of *A Time to Choose*.

	1985 Projection (Quads)
"Reference Energy Systems (RES) and Resource Data" prepared for the Office of Science and Technology by Brookhaven National Laboratory, April 1972.	117

	1985 Projection (Quads)
W. G. Dupree and J. A. West, "U.S. Energy Through the Year 2000," U.S. Department of Interior, December 1972	117
The Base Case projections of the "Project Independence Report," Federal Energy Administration, November 1974[a]	
with imports @ $ 4/barrel	118
with imports @ $ 7/barrel	110
with imports @ $11/barrel	103

The RES model has been widely used by the AEC and subsequently by ERDA in developing self-consistent supply/demand projections. In this model future energy demand is disaggregated in key areas for selected years, out to the year 2020. The RES model was used recently in ERDA–48 to show how energy would be used with alternative projections. The model is based on extrapolating end uses and trends in end uses established in the well-known Stanford Research Institute report ("Patterns of Energy Consumption in the United States," prepared by Stanford Research Institute for the Office of Science and Technology, January 1972), with projections based on various studies in the literature relating to specific end uses. The RES projection essentially reflects a continuation of historical demand growth trends, coupled to a continuing shift toward electrification.

It is curious that for a Department of Interior projection the authors of the critique chose to list a high 1971 projection, while mentioning only in a dismissive footnote the more recent and widely cited Dupree-West projection, which is about the same as the EPP Historical Growth projection. The Dupree-West projection envisions very rapid growth in GNP (4.3 percent per year to 1980 and 4.0 percent thereafter) and a flattening out of the long-term downward

---

[a]Interestingly, with two more years of experience and data, the FEA update to the Project Independence Report, "The National Energy Outlook, 1976," gave the following 1985 projections for its reference case (in Quads):

with imports @ $ 6/barrel	103
with imports @ $13/barrel	99
with imports @ $16/barrel	97

Also, the recent ERDA base case projection ("Creating Energy Choices for the Future, Volume 1: The Plan," ERDA–48, June 28, 1975) envisions 107 Quads for U.S. energy consumption in 1985.

trend in the energy/GNP ratio, both assumptions which tend to increase future energy demand.

It is also strange that the authors of the critique chose to ignore the Project Independence Report in their list, as that study has the distinction of involving perhaps the greatest commitment of dollar and human resources of any energy study. The high 1985 projection of that report, based on the pre-embargo price for imported oil, is practically the same as that of EPP's Historical Growth scenario. While the study can be criticized in many respects, it is a far more sophisticated study than most of the studies listed in table 5-1 of the critique.

One of the entries in that table suggests a 1985 projection of 124 Quads made in 1973 by the Council on Environmental Quality. The only 1973 CEQ publication involving energy projections was the report "Energy and the Environment: Electric Power," released in August, 1973. This report does not set forth CEQ projections but instead looks at the environmental impacts of the Dupree-West projections. In fact, the CEQ energy projection issued the next year ("A National Energy Conservation Program: the Half and Half Plan," March 1974) envisions energy growth to the year 2000 at 1.8 percent per year, which is the same as the EPP Technical Fix projection.

It should also be pointed out that the conservation scenario projections by FEA and ERDA are close to those projected by EPP for the Technical Fix scenario:

	1985 Projection (Quads)
Technical Fix Scenario	92
Project Independence Report	
with imports @ $ 7/barrel	99
with imports @ $11/barrel	94
National Energy Outlook, 1976	
with imports @ $ 8/barrel	97
with imports @ $13/barrel	93
with imports @ $16/barrel	92
ERDA-48	97

All this discussion shows that there were several major studies during the period of the Energy Policy Project with base case energy projections close to those of the Historical Growth scenario. Moreover, with higher prices these base case projections gave considerably lower 1985 energy consumption. Also, these studies show energy budgets comparable to those of the TF scenario when specific conservation policies were considered.

It is important to put the discussion of "historical growth" into a broader context than that put forth by the Mobil authors. The EPP Historical Growth projection of 2.7 percent annual growth in per capita energy use for 1972 to 1985 is roughly consistent with the 1960-72 average per capita growth rate of 2.8 percent per year, whereas the Mobil "Historical Growth" projection involves a higher annual growth pace of 3.6 percent. But it is noteworthy that the 1960-72 period was a narrow and perhaps anomalous slice of history, when the real price of energy was declining and per capita energy growth was unusually high. The average per capita energy growth rate for both 1900-1972 and 1945-1972 was only 1.4 percent per year. In the period 1945 to 1960 per capita energy use increased hardly at all. Thus, the Mobil argument that energy savings estimates for 1985 should be made relative to a baseline 1985 energy demand of 133 quadrillion BTU/year is based on the acceleration of a growth rate that was already unusually high compared to long-term historical trends.

Further, a recently completed and unusually comprehensive analysis of expected future growth in energy and GNP prepared for the U.S. Energy Research and Development Administration suggests that the EPP Historical Growth scenario *over* rather than *under* estimated the likely future rate of growth of energy use now in prospect. This study, "US Energy and Economic Growth, 1975-2010," was prepared by the Institute for Energy Analysis, Oak Ridge Associated Universities, Oak Ridge, Tennessee, and released in September 1976.

Table B-1 shows the high and low projection of IEA compared with the projections of EPP and NPC. The IEA analysis strongly suggests that likely trends in the economy are already moving us towards a low-energy regime. The IEA characterizes the estimates as follows:

> The low estimates that emerge from our analysis are in no sense "normative;" we have avoided suggesting what *ought* to be the U.S. energy future. Rather, our estimates flow from an analysis of what we believe is likely to happen in a surprise-free world. Both our high and low scenarios for long-term GNP growth are optimistic in the sense that we have used optimistic assumptions concerning future productivity gains. In general, we have tried to bias results toward the high side. For example, we have used optimistic assumptions about future labor productivity and have been conservative in our judgments regarding future energy conservation.

Table B-1. Projected Energy Growth

	Energy Consumption (Quads)		GNP Annual Growth Rate (Percent)	
	1985	2000	1975–85	1985–2000
IEA				
High	88	126	3.6	3.0
Low	82	101	3.6	2.7
EPP				
Historical Growth	116	187	3.6	3.3
Technical Fix	92	124	3.5	3.1
Zero Energy Growth	88	100	3.5	3.1
NPC				
High	130	—	4.4	—
Intermediate	125	—	4.2	—
Low	113	—-	3.2	—

DID THE EPP REALLY UNDERESTIMATE SIGNIFICANT COMPONENTS OF ENERGY DEMAND?

Housing Projections: The authors of the critique say the EPP estimate of 80 million occupied housing units in 1985 is too low. Any forecast must be evaluated in terms of its consistency with the assumptions underlying it, and the credence to be given to these assumptions. EPP projections for population, housing units, labor force, etc., were developed for the EPP through contract by a technology assessment group at George Washington University. Population projections were based on the Census Bureau's "Series E" population projection as revised in December 1972. The Census Bureau's housing series was utilized in developing household projections. Alternatively 84 or 82 million units (based on series 1 and series 2 household projections respectively of the Census Bureau's *Current Population Reports*, series P-25, No. 476, February 1972) could have been used for occupied housing projections. If the higher of these alternative projections should prove to be correct, and energy use were simply proportional to the number of houses, the Historical Growth residential housing energy budget could be low by 1.1 Quads and the Technical Fix budget by 0.9 Quads, all other factors being equal. However, this is an upper limit for the increase, because a large share of the increased number of households would be single working-age persons living in apartments, who would be away from their apartment much of the day, thus consuming much less energy than the average household. The Project Independence Report analysis for residential energy demand, carried out by Arthur D. Little, Inc., is based on 84 million occupied housing units in 1985 and shows 20.5 Quads for residential energy consumption in the base case, compared to 22.9 Quads in the EPP report. Thus, differences in estimates of the number of occupied housing units in 1985 need not result in proportional differences in household energy use.

Commercial Area. The critique argues that the EPP projection of commercial space growing in proportion to the number of service sector employees is unrealistic. At the time the EPP work was done data on commercial space were not readily available, so this formula was adopted as reasonable. Subsequently, however, a study of commercial space projections has been carried out ("Residential and Commercial Energy Use Patterns, 1970-1990," prepared by the Interagency Task Force on Energy Conservation, *Project Independence Report*, November 1974). That study showed: 21,610 million square feet of commercial area in 1970; removals for the period 1970-85 estimated at 4560 million square feet; and new construction area A estimated in terms of disposable income I (in billions of 1958 $) by A = -220 + 1.45I. For 1970, I = $508 billion. Using the EPP/DRI average annual growth rate of 3.7 percent for real disposable income (see appendix F of *A Time to Choose*) in the Project Independence Report model yields new construction amounting to 11,480 million square feet in the period 1970-85. Thus, in 1985 commercial area would amount to 28,530 million square feet, which is 1.32 times the 1970 value. The simpler EPP model estimated 1985 commercial area to be 1.35 times the 1970 value (see table A-4, page 439 of *A Time to Choose*).

Number of Automobiles: The authors of the critique say the EPP estimate of 119 million autos by 1985 is too low by *at least* 6 million autos. In contrast, the NPC report they prefer envisions 140 million autos. The source of the EPP estimate is the Federal Highway Administration estimate of 123 million autos for a population of 245 million, corrected for a lower population. (See A. French, et al., "Highway Travel Forecasts Related to Energy Requirements," Federal Highway Administration, December 1972.) If instead the EPP had adopted the unmodified FHA projection of 123 million autos, the Historical Growth and Technical Fix energy budgets would have been higher by about 0.4 Quads and 0.3 Quads respectively. Of course, without a wholly planned economy there is no "correct" projection of the number of automobiles or houses, but the NPC number appears to overestimate historical trends, as perceived by the agency responsible for understanding evolving trends, by some 17 million cars. This is equivalent to about 2 Quads of extra energy in the NPC total. The effect is even more exaggerated when all motor vehicles (cars, trucks, and buses) are considered; in this case, the NPC envisions 178 million vehicles, compared to 151 million projected by the FHA, corresponding to a higher total highway fuel estimate of perhaps 3 Quads for 1985.

The Use of Automobiles. The critique argues that the EPP was not justified in assuming that cars would be driven only 10,000 miles per year on the average. This number was chosen on the basis of the observation that, since the end of World War II, the average number of miles driven per year per car has varied from 9500 by no more than ±5 percent. While it is true that this number began rising steadily in the late 1960s, the rate of increase slowed considerably as the 10,000 miles level was approached and dropped sharply in the recession year of 1974, the last year for which data are available (Figure B-1). Why cars are driven as much as they are is not well understood. The critique suggests that fuel price is an important factor so that more efficient cars might be driven more. But the time available for driving is likely to be a more important factor, and this would not change with fuel prices or car efficiency. In any event,

Figure B-1. Annual Automobile Use

it seems unlikely that increased fuel efficiency will totally compensate for higher fuel prices.

Environmental Protection. The critique, citing the NPC, suggests that the pursuit of environmental quality goals is a significant factor in driving up the growth rate for energy. The NPC projected that environmental protection measures will account for 4.4 to 6.2 Quads of energy use by 1985. A study carried out for the EPP (J. Davidson et al., "Energy Needs for Pollution Control, "in *The Energy Conservation Papers*, R. H. Williams, ed., Ballinger, 1975) shows that pursuit of environmental goals under historical growth conditions would result by 1985 in an energy penalty of only 2.3 Quads. The EPP study concluded that the NPC had to include under the rubric "pollution control" a broad definition of provision and disposal of water to get the large penalty for sewage and fresh water treatment they obtained.

The critique further states that pollution control measures invariably lead to greater energy requirements. But the NPC calculation seems to ignore the fact that there are opportunities for pollution control which actually lead to less energy use:

1. The EPP study ("Energy Needs for Pollution Control") points out that solid waste disposal can result in an energy credit instead of a debit when organic wastes are used as fuel. (The Mobile critique suggests that the net pollution control energy penalty estimated for 1985 in this study involves a credit for recovering energy from crop residues. This is incorrect. Credit was not taken for this potential energy resource simply because crop residues do not present a waste disposal problem.)

2. Another EPP study (E. P. Gyftopoulos et al., *Potential Fuel Effectiveness in Industry*, Ballinger, 1974) describes a process developed to reduce water pollution in the paper industry, a by-product of which was a reduction of the fuel demand for paper making by one-half.

3. When electricity is produced as a by-product of industrial steam generation, thermal pollution can be virtually eliminated because no cooling water is needed when the waste heat is utilized. An added benefit is that air pollution is reduced from what it would be if steam and electricity where produced separately, since less fuel is required.

Moreover, where there are energy penalties for pollution control, forces of innovation will tend to reduce the magnitude of the penalty over time. We are already seeing this for automotive pollution controls. The most reliable studies suggest an average energy penalty for pollution control of 10.1 to 13.6 percent for 1973 automobiles. The EPP study ("Energy Needs for Pollution Control") estimated the penalty for 1975 cars with catalytic converters to be only about 5 percent. Similarly, engineering improvements such as certain stratified charge engines and lightweight diesels would lead to improved fuel economy while meeting emissions standards. In general, pollution control will result in much less of an energy penalty when pollution control is a design feature of the technology instead of a retrofitted fix.

WHAT ABOUT THOSE ELECTRIC HEATING PROJECTIONS?

Space Heating. The critique accuses the EPP of setting up a straw man with its high estimate of electric resistance heating for the HG scenario. They point out that the NPC estimate of electrically heated houses is far less than what EPP assumed. But the oil industry (NPC) and the electric utility industry have very different views of historical growth, and the authors of the critique have clearly failed to grasp certain key aspects of historical growth in the use of electricity. The EPP projection for residential space heating is equivalent to that set forth by *Electrical World* ("24th Annual Electric Industry Forecast," 15 September 1973). The projected growth in electric space heating was not restricted to new construction, as the critique suggests. Indeed *Electrical World* ("23rd Annual Electric Industry Forecast," 15 September 1972) envisioned that during the 1980s about half of all electrically heated homes would be conversions.

Why the wide difference between the NPC and *Electrical World* regarding the potential for electric resistive heat? The answer appears to be that the utility industry at that time perceived increased opportunities for electric resistive heat because of expectations of continued decline in the real price of electricity. Historically, electric power growth has been so rapid in large part because in real terms electricity prices have fallen dramatically over time compared to other goods and services, including, for example, fuel oil. Figures B-2 and B-3 show[b] that while in real terms the retail price of home heating oil changed hardly at all from 1940 to 1970, the price of residential electricity declined at an average rate of 5½ percent

[b]The prices for both residential electricity and fuel oil in these figures were converted to constant dollars using as a deflator the consumer price index. For industrial electricity the deflator used is the wholesale price index for industrial commodities. Average electricity prices (in current $) were obtained from Edison Electric Institute sources. Fuel oil prices (in current $) were obtained from *Retail Prices and Indexes of Fuels and Electricity*, compiled by the U.S. Bureau of Labor Statistics (see also *Statistical Abstract.*)

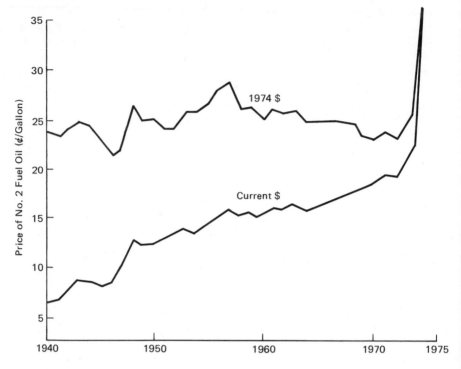

Figure B-2.   Retail Price of No. 2 Fuel Oil

per year. In the past improvements in generating efficiency and scale economies led to these dramatic price reductions. Until recently, it was expected that nuclear power with its cheap fuel would enable this trend to continue. If the price of residential electricity had continued to decline at the 1960s average rate of 4 percent per year the result by 1985 would have been that electric resistive heat could compete with oil at 36¢/gallon on a straight BTU equivalent basis (i.e., without taking credit for the added comfort, cleanliness, and convenience of electric over oil heat or without taking credit for any capital cost advantage of electric units over oil furnaces).

Thus, the expectation of a continually improving price for electricity relative to fuel oil reflects historical trends and means that over time electricity for space heating would become more and more competitive, even outside the mild climate areas (the South) or the low-cost electricity areas (the Pacific Northwest and the TVA region) where most electrically heated homes have been located in the past. The historical trend toward increasing competitiveness of electric heat in mild climates is indicated by the fact that the percentage of all electrically heated houses located in the Northeast and the North

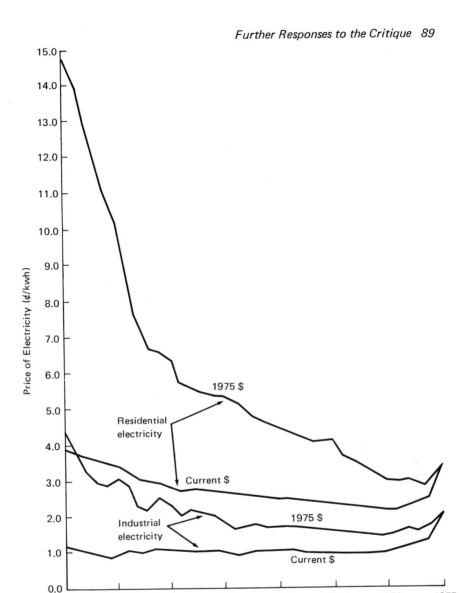

Figure B-3.   Average Electricity Prices in the U.S.

Central regions of the country increased from 8 percent in 1960 to 21 percent in 1970. (John Tansil, "Residential Consumption of Electricity, 1950–1970," Oak Ridge National Laboratory report ORNL-NSF-EP-51, July 1973.)

The trend toward lower electricity prices also tended to increase the average use of electricity for space heating, from 10,000 KWH per household in 1950, to 12,900 in 1960, and to 14,600 in 1970. In part this increased consumption per unit reflects the penetration of moderate climate markets. But such increases took place even within specific regions; between 1960 and 1970 usage per household in the South increased from 12,100 to 14,900 KWH (John Tansil, op. cit.). In the EPP HG projection,[c] average space heating electricity use per household in 1985 is 17,500 KWH, corresponding to a continuation of the historical rate of increase, from 1960 to 1970, of 1.2 percent per year. For comparison, per household electricity consumption in milder climates averaged in 1970 18,800 KWH in New England, 16,900 KWH in the Middle Atlantic region, 22,200 KWH in the East North Central region, 20,000 KWH in the West North Central region, and 16,200 KWH in the Mountain region (S. H. Dole, "Energy Use and Conservation in the Residential Sector: A Regional Analysis," RAND Corporation report R-1641-NSF, June 1975). For historical growth conditions the EPP projected substantial penetration of electrical heating in these regions.

Present events, however, have caused these expectations to change. Today the power industry expects the price of electricity (in real terms) to *rise* by more than 2 percent per year over the next decade; thus, by 1985, oil would have to cost more than $1.00 per gallon for resistive heat to be competitive. In recognition of this fact, *Electrical World* reduced its 1985 resistive space heating projection by 35 percent between September 15, 1973 and September 15, 1975. Most of this reduction reflects the expectation not of fewer electrically heated homes but rather a more frugal use of electric heat, either through use of heat pumps or through reduced heat losses. *Electrical World* ("27th Annual Electric Industry Forecast," 15 September 1976) points out that in 1975 electric heat was

---

[c]The authors of the critique assert: "The Project staff began with an estimate of 1970 space heating consumption which is two and a half times the estimate of respected authorities in the field." But in fact the EPP report does not explicitly contain a statement of electricity consumption for space heating in 1970. Moreover, the level of electricity usage for space heating in 1970 cited in the NPC report (upon which the authors of the critique are relying as their authoritative source) is so low relative to the level estimated in the principal references on residential electricity use that it is understandable how it was difficult for the authors of the critique to observe true "historical trends." In table 33, p. 122, of *U.S. Energy Outlook; Energy Demand*, National Petroleum Council, it is stated that electricity consumption for residential space heating in 1970 was 39.6×10^9 KWH. Electrical industry sources and independent analysts have estimated a much higher level of about 70×10^9 KWH. (67.3×10^9 KWH is given in "The 26th Annual Electrical Industry Forecast," *Electrical World*, 15 September 1975; 71.2×10^9 KWH is given by John Tansil, "Residential Consumption of Electricity, 1950-1970," Oak Ridge National Laboratory Report ORNL-NSF-EP-51, July 1973; and 66.6×10^9 KWH is given by S. H. Dole, "Energy Use and Conservation in the Residential Sector: A Regional Analysis," RAND Corporation report R-1641-NSF, June 1975.)

installed in 60 percent and 70 percent of new single-family and multifamily housing construction respectively and projects that these shares will rise to 80 percent and 90 percent by the mid 1980s.

The critique makes the same point about the EPP assumption of rapid growth in resistive space heat in the commercial sector. The response is essentially the same as above for the residential case. The RES model* projected an even higher value than EPP for resistive space heat in the commercial sector in 1985, although the total resistive space heat projection for the combined residential/commercial sectors is the same in the RES model and the Historical Growth scenario.

Industrial Process Heat. The authors of the critique say that the EPP projection of growth in electricity for industrial process heat is much too high. As in the case of resistive space heat, the EPP projection might not make sense in light of present electricity prices or in light of today's expectations about future electricity prices. But with the expectation of a continued historical price decline of 2.5 to 3 percent per year, industrial electricity prices would have fallen from an average of 1.17¢/KWH in 1973 to 0.87¢/KWH or less in 1985. Taking into account that all the electrical heat can be delivered to process, but not all the heat from burning fuel directly, this means that electricity could compete with oil at under $10/barrel, even without taking credit for capital cost advantages of electricity use, and even without a discount price for high volume direct heat applications. This attractive price, expectations of gas scarcity, and the convenience of electricity over coal are all factors that could lead to a large demand for electricity in direct heat applications under true "historical growth" conditions. The EPP Historical Growth projection of industrial resistive heat for 2000 is about the same as that in the RES model and is only about two-thirds of that projected in the "intensive electrification" scenario of ERDA–48, *Creating Energy Choices*, 1975.

HOW REALISTIC ARE THE EPP ESTIMATES OF POTENTIAL ENERGY SAVINGS?

Residential: The critique argues that the example of fuel savings from thermally tightening a new home, as given on page 48 of *A Time to Choose*, is too great and is inconsistent with the savings shown in appendix A, p. 434. There is no inconsistency. The 20 percent difference in heat losses in appendix A is the assumed *average* for TF vs. HG houses built in the period 1975–85. The example on page 48 is for a *fully* insulated new house relative to an

*"Reference Energy Systems (RES) and Resource Data," prepared for the Office of Science and Technology by Brookhaven National Laboratory, April 1972.

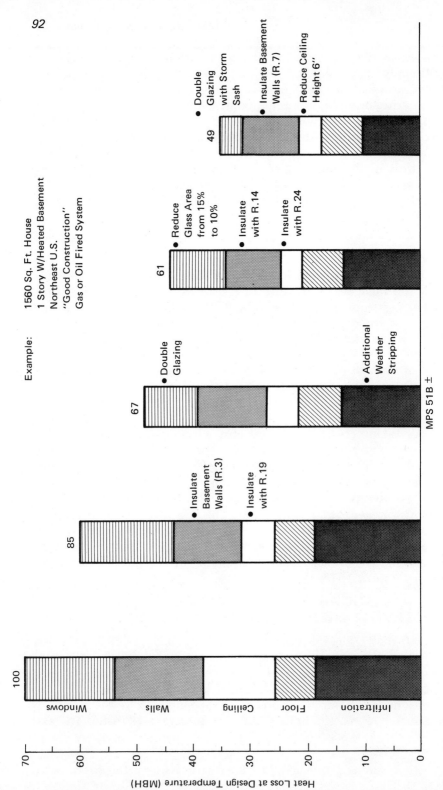

Figure B-4. Effect of Selected House Modifications on Space Heating Requirements

Source: "Residential and Commercial Energy Use Patterns 1970–1990," prepared by the Interagency Task Force on Conservation,

existing house, in New York. The 50 percent savings quoted here are in line with other estimates (Figures B-4 and B-5; table B-2).

Overall EPP projects 18.2 Quads for the residential sector in 1985. This level is the same as what would result from the Project Independence Report analysis if half of the "maximum" potential reductions based on current reasonable technology and cost were implemented.

Here, as elsewhere, it appears that as more is learned about conservation the opportunities seem to expand. At the time of the Project the "conventional wisdom" about opportunities for reducing fuel consumption for space heating in existing houses was that perhaps a one-quarter fuel savings would be possible, but now it appears

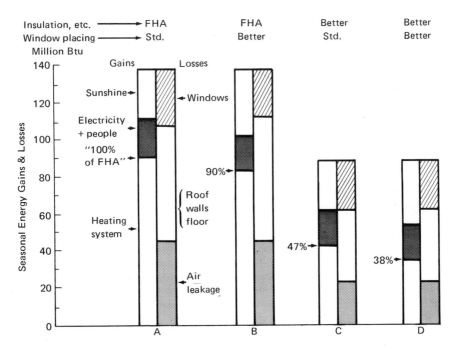

Figure B-5. Four Variations in a Conventional House

Calculated heating energy requirements for variations in window placement and allowable heat losses: (A) standard window placement and standard FHA allowable heat losses: (B) 80 square feet of window shifted from north to south side of house. (C) better than standard allowable heat losses with standard window placement. (D) better window placement and better than standard allowable heat losses.

Source: R. W. Bliss, "Why Not Just Build the House Right in the First Place," *Bulletin of the Atomic Scientists*, March 1976.

Table B–2. Summary of Energy Savings for New Residential Construction

56 million BTU saved by going from standard FHA allowable heat losses and standard window placement to better than standard allowable heat losses and better window placement

Item	Seasonal Saving (million Btu)	How Achieved
Less air infiltration	22	Infiltration reduced from 1 air change per hour to one-half air change per hour, by tighter construction
Less floor loss	12	Better perimeter insulation
Less wall loss	7	Wall U-value changed from 0.085 to 0.065
Increased solar gain	7	80 square feet of window shifted from north to south side of house
Less window loss	5	Window U-value changed from 0.65 to 0.54
Less door loss	$\dfrac{3}{56}$	Storm doors at all exits

Source: R. W. Bliss, "Why Not Just Build the House Right in the First Place," *Bulletin of the Atomic Scientists,* March 1976.

that greater savings may in fact be achievable. Drawing on closely monitored experience over the last four years in townhouses in Twin Rivers, New Jersey, Robert Socolow reported that after a first round of economical retrofit measures in these houses, fuel savings of one-third relative to pre oil embargo use patterns were realized on the average for space heating ("Energy Conservation in Existing Residences: Your Home Deserves a House Call," presented at the *Conference on Energy Efficiency as a National Priority,* 20 May 1976, Washington, D.C.). Moreover, savings up to one-half or even more are expected from the second round of planned retrofit measures. It is, of course, not surprising that new conservation technologies seem to be emerging rapidly, since in the era of low-cost energy there was so little incentive to save or to innovate to save.

Transportation: The authors of the critique feel that the estimates EPP sets forth for auto fuel economy improvements (see p. 59 of *A Time to Choose*) are speculative. These estimates were based on a federal assessment of the potential for automobile fuel economy improvements ("Research and Development Opportunities for Improved Transportation Energy Usage," carried out by the Transportation Energy Panel for 1972 Energy R&D Goals Study of the Office of Science and Technology) and on an Alcoa study (ref. 5 in chapter 3 of *A Time to Choose*) assessing the potential for using aluminum in auto manufacture to reduce fuel consumption. The improved fuel economy judged feasible is in agreement with the results of a major study of opportunities for improved automotive fuel economy carried out in the summer of 1974 under the auspices of the American Physical Society (published as *Efficient Use of Energy: Part I, A Physics Perspective*). The APS study found that with today's technology (reoptimization of engine size, radial tires, modest streamlining, and a 20 percent weight reduction) the fuel economy of an average-sized auto could be increased to 20 mpg. Moreover, the APS study showed that with some technological innovations cars in the 1980s and beyond could be getting a 30–35 mpg. Of course some small cars have this fuel economy today.

The critique suggests that pursuing this fuel economy improvement strategy would make larger, safer cars unavailable. However, as the above studies show, substantial fuel economy improvements could be obtained through modest technical changes that do not require reducing the average car size to that of a subcompact. Also, the proposed fuel economy standard was for an industry average, i.e., a mix of large, medium, and small-sized cars.

The critique's authors find incredible the EPP proposal that by the end of the century there could be a significant shift of short-haul (less than 400 mile) intercity passenger travel from air to more efficient rapid rail transport. Rail passenger traffic in this shift would increase from 11 billion passenger miles in 1970 to 108 billion passenger miles in 2000. To put these numbers in perspective, it is worth noting that rail passenger traffic in the U.S. hit its peak of 96 billion passenger miles in the wartime year of 1944. Moreover, between 1950 and 1970 air passenger traffic increased from 9 to 110 billion passenger miles. Also, the projected railroad passenger travel for 2000 amounts to only 400 miles per capita per year, which is less than one Washington, D.C.–New York round trip. For comparison per capita auto and air travel would be 9600 and 3900 miles respectively in the Technical Fix scenario in 2000 (compared to 8300 and 800 miles respectively in 1970).

For this rail travel EPP assumed an energy intensity of 1000 BTU/passenger mile, which again the authors of the critique find incredible. This EPP estimate was obtained from a study of future transportation systems (Richard Rice, "Toward More Transportation with Less Energy," *Technology Review*, February 1974, p. 45). This value implies a significant efficiency improvement over the present energy intensity of 2900 BTU/PM. But even if no improvement over present practice could be achieved, U.S. energy requirements would hardly be affected (up only 0.2 Quads in 2000). It is worth noting also that in Rice's transportation model rail passenger travel in the year 2000 is projected to be 350 billion passenger miles, or more than three times what EPP assumed for the TF scenario.

The critique suggests that EPP did not consider the energy required to rebuild and expand the railroads. But EPP did in fact commission a study (Bruce Hannon et al., "Energy, Employment, and Dollar Impacts of Alternative Transportation Options," in *The Energy Conservation Paper*, R. H. Williams, ed.) to examine such questions. This study found that, on a per passenger mile basis, the total energy for rail transportation (direct energy purchases plus indirect energy for equipment manufacture, construction of terminals, etc.) amounts to 1.7 times the direct energy, and for air transport the total energy is 1.4 times the direct energy. This study also found that on the same basis indirect energy for air travel is 1.3 times that for railroads. Thus, there is both a direct and a (modest) indirect energy saving associated with rebuilding railroads instead of further expansion of air travel capacity.

The critique claims that in the case of air transport the EPP conservation measures would sharply curtail growth in both passenger and freight traffic and that EPP gave no attention to considerations of time and convenience in proposing shifts from air to rail or air to truck or truck to rail for intercity transport. Yet *both* the HG and TF scenarios involve a doubling of air passenger traffic and a tripling of freight traffic by 1985. By 2000 the shift of short-haul air passenger traffic to rapid rail envisioned for the TF scenario involved only 10 percent of the domestic air travel projected for the HG scenario. Similarly, a shift of only 10 percent of domestic air freight volume to truck and rail was envisioned. In absolute terms the air passenger and freight volumes envisioned for the TF scenario in 2000 would be respectively four and nine fold higher than in 1975.

Also, time *was* regarded by EPP as a pivotal factor (see p. 448 of *A Time to Choose*) in judging whether a particular shift made sense or not:

1. Only short-haul (less than 400 miles) air trips were assumed to shift from air to rapid rail in the TF scenario by 2000. Point-to-point travel time for rapid rail would likely be comparable to or even less than that for air for such trips.
2. For similar time considerations it was assumed that air freight trips less than 250 miles would be shifted to truck and that trips of 250 to 400 mile length would be shifted to rail. For longer hauls the air freight tonnage is the same in the HG and TF scenarios.
3. The shifts from truck to rail transport were considered likely only for long hauls (longer than 500 miles by 1985) and only for competitive cargo. For example, EPP assumed 20 percent of combination truck traffic is shifted to rail by 1985. A DOT study shows that with modest policy changes over half of intercity truck freight could be shifted to rail. See p. 451 of *A Time to Choose* for details.

Industrial: The critique chides the EPP for insufficient documentation of potential energy savings in the industrial area under the category "miscellaneous." The potential savings in the industrial sector can be estimated two ways: by process (process steam, direct heat, feedstocks, electrolytic, etc.) or by product (steel, paper, glass, etc.). For five selected industries for which available data were related to output, EPP estimated savings *by product*. For the rest of manufacturing EPP estimated potential savings *by process* (the "miscellaneous" categories shown on p. 461). This approach to industrial energy conservation is common to many other studies. "Belt tightening" refers to better management practices and no changes in capital equipment. Savings on the order of 15 percent throughout industry for such good housekeeping measures have been estimated by others (Charles Berg, "Conservation in Industry," *Science*, 19 April 1974, and "Energy Conservation Program Guide for Industry and Commerce," NBS Handbook 115, NBS, September 1974). For the miscellaneous categories referred to, EPP estimates for 1985 a more modest 9 percent savings. Miscellaneous industria. energy savings via heat recuperation were based on research carried out for EPP (E.P. Gyftopoulos et al., *Potential for Fuel Effectiveness in Industry*, Ballinger, 1974).

The authors of the critique seem to be particularly disturbed by the EPP fuel-savings estimates for cogeneration, i.e., the production of electricity as a by-product of industrial process steam generation. The technology is important for conservation because the fuel required to produce a kilowatt hour of cogenerated electricity, beyond what is needed to produce process steam, is often less than half what is required at a central station power plant. An added benefit is that with an emphasis on cogeneration rather than central station power generation it would be easier to adjust electricity supply to evolving uncertain electricity demand and thereby minimize potential overcapacity. This flexibility results from the relatively small scale of cogeneration plants that can be brought on line in two to three years compared to the six to ten year lead times for central station plants.

The EPP estimate of 0.9 Quads fuel savings for 1985 from cogeneration (0.4 in the "miscellaneous" category and the rest in the industries listed in table A-13, p. 460, of *A Time to Choose*) was based on EPP research (*Potential for Fuel Effectiveness in Industry*). The conservative judgment was made that retrofit opportunities would not be great. Subsequent and much more exhaustive studies indicate that EPP greatly underestimated the cogeneration potential. One 1975 study ("Energy Industrial Center Study" prepared by Dow Chemical Company, ERI of Michigan, Townsend-Greenspan and Co., and Cravath Swaine and Moore, for the National Science Foundation, June 1975) estimated that if economics were the only determining factor some 1.4 Quads could be saved with cogeneration by 1985. One of the shortcomings of the Dow study is that it considered only the steam turbine cycle for which the cogeneration potential is fairly limited, and it did not look at the relative economics of industry vs. utility ownership of onsite generation units or at the economics under alternative taxation policies or financing schemes. A more recent study ("A Study of Inplant Electric Power Generation in the Chemical, Petroleum Refining and Paper and Pulp Industries," a report prepared by Thermo Electron Corporation for the Federal Energy Administration, June 1976) takes these factors into account and estimates for the chemical, petroleum refining, and paper and pulp industries even more substantial opportunities for economic savings:

	1985 Savings Potential *(Quads)*	
	With Utility Ownership	*With Industry Ownership*
With Steam Turbines	0.9–1.0	0.5–0.9
With Gas Turbines	3.4–3.5	2.1–3.2
With Diesels	4.2–4.8	2.0–4.0

In each category here economic savings potential varies (especially with industrial ownership) according to the level of the incentive (tax credit).

These more recent studies show that EPP was, if anything, overly conservative in estimating the cogeneration potential. The barriers to cogeneration, as pointed out by EPP, are neither technological nor economic. They are institutional. That cogeneration technology would be more widely used under more favorable institutional arrangements is suggested by a comparison of U.S. to West German experience: while only 4 percent of U.S. electricity is produced this way today, cogeneration accounts for about 12 percent of West Germany's electrical generating capacity.

In most cases economic operation requires interconnection with the utility. To capture scale sconomies cogeneration electricity should be produced near the limit set by the size of the steam load. In many cases this means producing more power than can be consumed on site. Hence, the utility should be willing to buy this excess electricity at a fair price. Also, back-up capacity provided by the utility would in many instances be cheaper than on-site back-up capacity, since this way many firms could share a common back-up capacity. Unfortunately, utility pricing policies for back-up power (high demand charges and declining block rates), whether justified or not by cost of service, and an unwillingness to buy cogeneration electricity have inhibited this technology.

Because there are substantial public benefits from cogeneration beyond the potential benefits to the utility and the firm involved, regulatory actions are called for. Public utility commissions would have to require interconnection between utilities and cogenerating firms in order to break the barriers to this technology.

The Implementation Schedules for Conservation: The critique suggests that EPP did not give attention to the problem of time frame for the implementation of industrial conservation measures. Yet note (a) to table A-11 on page 458 of *A Time to Choose* shows that EPP did indeed take into account the time required for capital equipment turnover:

> Energy requirements for 1985 represent the average for a mix of some plants with present technology plus other plants using the improved technologies described in the Thermo Electron Study. For these industries, we assume that all new productive capacity after 1980 (including that which replaced old capacity retired at a rate of 2 percent per year) uses

the improved technology. We assume that the energy efficiency of old capacity improves at a rate of 1.3 percent per year through various "leak plugging" measures.

There are also cases in a given plant where conservation is so attractive that it may be desirable to retire existing inefficient equipment early in favor of more efficient technology. The recent Dow and Thermo Electron studies cited above suggest that EPP significantly underestimated such opportunities for cogeneration. For example, in discussing coal-fired cogeneration opportunities, Dow's "Energy Industrial Center Study" points out: "If a company owned an (oil-fired) package boiler six years old in 1980, it could still achieve a 93 percent return (before tax) on the investment in a new coal-fired boiler to replace the oil-fired one." This change is economic even though package boilers ordinarily last fifteen years. In other cases there are retrofit opportunities that require only relatively minor changes in existing plants.

SOME MISCELLANEOUS AND SPECIFIC ITEMS

Residential/Commercial Sectors. 1. The critique challenges the value of the EPP recommendation that building codes be revised so that new buildings would be more energy efficient, claiming:

> This revision would ignore local and regional economic incentives. in the residential sector, and would place on all citizens the burden of higher initial construction costs . . . . This would work extreme hardships on citizens in lower income brackets, where frequently the size of the down payment and the monthly mortgage payments determine whether or not a family can own its own home.

The EPP points out that building codes are needed to facilitate life-cycle costing. The free market may work less effectively here, because without codes the typical builder-developer, who is often strapped for capital, has had little incentive to invest a little extra to reduce operating costs for the future homeowner. The EPP recommended: "The existing system of direct state and local regulation of building design through building codes should be maintained in view of climatic and other regional variations in building design environment" (p. 55). Thus, the EPP proposal does not ignore "local and regional economic incentives" as the critique suggests.

It is certainly true, as the critique claims, that more energy efficient housing would cost more. However, the proposal is to pursue only those investments that would be economical on a life-cycle cost basis. The EPP estimated that some $120 billion would be needed for conservation investments in the residential sector in the period 1975–2000. This works out to an average of about $1200 per household, which the critique suggest would work extreme hardship on citizens in lower-income brackets. However, this investment would be spread out over twenty-five years and would be more than offset by reduced fuel costs. But the fact remains that many lower-income homeowners do not have ready access to the capital resources needed for these investments. Since making the capital more available for conservation investments would serve the broader national interest by reducing the total capital requirements for energy, the EPP report recommended that "steps should be taken to provide lower income homeowners with subsidized guaranteed loans to allow them to improve the energy efficiency of their homes."

2. The critique also states that the EPP had no significant empirical data and conducted no field surveys regarding fuel use in the existing housing stock to provide the basis for judging the impact of conservation measures. On the contrary, the EPP commissioned a major study (*The American Energy Consumer* by D. K. Newman and Dawn Day, Ballinger, 1975) which involved the first significant national survey of energy consumption habits in the U.S. The authors, at the Washington Center for Metropolitan Studies, carried out with the assistance of Response Analysis Corporation a national survey (a probability sample of 1455 households throughout the U.S.) to ascertain how Americans use energy. The survey obtained much statistical information about the size and characteristics of homes and energy information such as type of fuel used, quantity consumed, whether or not there is insulation, the extent of storm window and weatherstripping use, and so on. This information was supplemented by an informal survey of representatives of the building industry carried out by EPP staff to estimate the degree of insulation for various ages of housing.

3. The authors of the critique chide the EPP for arbitrarily reducing the demand between the TF and ZEG scenarios for presently "unknown appliances" by up to 1.6 Quads in the year 2000. EPP included in the energy budgets for the HG and TF scenarios by the year 2000 a "phantom energy demand" that we could not foresee on the basis of present technological trends, a per household phantom demand equivalent to what an average household consumes for hot water heating or to what an average central air conditioner would use. This is a very generous estimate of potential "phantom demand"

because most opportunities for introducing new appliances into the home will likely be in areas like electronics and communications (e.g., home entertainment centers) which are not heavy energy users. For the ZEG scenario we assumed that because of the energy tax, a somewhat greater public concern about environmental impacts of energy use, less materialistic interest, etc., this phantom demand would be reduced about 45 percent. Nevertheless the ZEG phantom demand alone per household amounts to 10 percent of total household energy use today. This is in addition to all the "usual" amenities (including 100 percent saturation of dishwashers and central air conditioners).

Transportation. 1. From a comparison of the two tables on page 442 of *A Time to Choose*, the critique concludes that the EPP analysis regarding the number of automobiles and how much they are used is internally inconsistent. The table at the bottom of 442 was constructed to show one possible schedule for achieving an average fuel economy of 20 mpg by 1985. This schedule was developed from a DOT study of auto use by age. For the sample studied the average distance driven per year per car was 11,600 miles. In applying this model to the national average calculation shown in this table, the miles driven in a given year were renormalized to the 10,000 mile national average, which we obtained on the basis of FHA data. Through a clear clerical error, the numbers in the column "miles driven annually per car" were not reduced in the ratio 10/11.6 as they should have been. However, this oversight does not affect the result, which is the fuel economy schedule, nor does it affect the energy-savings calculation.

2. The authors of the critique feel that the projected growth in rail freight haulage for the TF scenario is unrealistic. This is a valid criticism. However, the real problem is not the difference between the Historical Growth and Technical Fix projections (the TF projection is only 13 percent greater than the HG projection in 2000). Rather, the HG projection is itself too high. In this case the EPP simply adopted the projection from the Brookhaven RES model. In light of more detailed information on expected future rail traffic now available ("Project Independence and Energy Conservation: Transportation Sectors," volume 2, FEA, November 1974) it appears that the projected ton mileage for Historical Growth in rail freight to the year 2000 should have been about 1500 billion instead of 2300 billion ton miles. Because of this, the HG energy demand in 2000 was *overestimated* by about 0.6 Quads.

Industry. It is true, as the critique says, that EPP did not explicitly show greater aluminum production for the TF scenario relative to the HG scenario to account for some 300 lb. of aluminum per car in the TF scenario. This was a dumb oversight; had this been done right, the TF energy demand in 1985 would have been greater by almost 0.2 Quads.

Energy Processing. 1. The critique's authors are puzzled about the calculation of the electric conversion efficiency for central station electric power plants for the scenarios. They were estimated on the following basis:

	HG Fuel Consumption in 1985 (Quads)	Efficiency (Percent)
Pre-1973 Fossil Fuel Plants	13.1	35
New Coal Plants	9.0	39
New Oil and Gas Plants	0.9	42
Nuclear Plants	10.0	33
	33.0	35.6

By 1985 the efficiency of the pre-1973 plants is improved through retiring old inefficient units (brought on line before 1955). The average for new coal plants includes efficient advanced cycles introduced in the early 1980s. New oil and gas cycles are assumed to be primarily combined cycle units (Brayton/Rankine cycles). It is noteworthy that the NPC report assumed that the average efficiency of combined cycle units would be more than 45 percent by 1985, very likely an overly optimistic assumption.

2. The authors of the critique feel that the EPP estimate of refinery efficient improvement is flawed because it does not take into account the different mixes of refinery output. However, the savings estimated depend mainly on the quantities of process steam and direct heat required on the average, with savings achieved through cogeneration, use of heat recuperators, and the like. The savings fraction used in the EPP calculations is an industry average rather than a value applicable for each plant. The EPP calculation is based on the EPP study (*Potential Fuel Effectiveness in Industry*), which explicitly took into account the variation of refinery efficiency with the mix of products, and estimated that by the early 1980s an

average savings of 25 percent could be achieved in petroleum re-fining. In its scenarios calculations of refinery losses for 1985 the EPP staff was more conservative, assuming only an 18 percent savings.

Index

About the Authors

William P. Tavoulareas is President of Mobil Corporation. After receiving degrees from St. John's University in business administration and in law, Mr. Tavoulareas became an accountant with Mobil Oil Corporation in 1947. He advanced to manager, Middle East affairs in 1958; manager, corporate planning and analysis department in 1959; vice president for plans and programs, International Division in 1961; and vice president of Mobil Oil for supply and distribution and international sales in 1963. He was senior vice president for Middle East Affairs, planning, supply, and transportation from 1965 to 1966, and Mobil Oil executive vice president and president of the North American Division from 1967 to 1969. Mr. Tavoulareas is a director of Mobil Corporation, Bankers Trust New York Corporation and Bankers Trust Company, General Foods Corporation, and Near East College Association. He is a trustee of Athens College, St. John's University, St. Paul's School, Long Island, and on the Board of Governors of New York Hospital.

Carl Kaysen is David W. Skinner Professor of Political Economy in the School of Humanities and Social Science at M.I.T. A former Director of the Institute for Advanced Study, Princeton, he did graduate work in economics at Harvard where he joined the economics faculty in 1950. He held the Lucius N. Littauer Chair of Political Economy at Harvard; was a Fulbright Visiting Professor at the London School of Economics, and a Guggenheim Fellow. Mr. Kaysen was Deputy Special Assistant for National Security Affairs during the Kennedy Administration, and has worked on a variety of public policy studies, such as Ford Foundation's Energy Policy Project and the Nuclear Energy Policy Study Group.